Do you want to hear a story?
Adventures in collective narrative practice

by David Denborough

Dulwich Centre Publications
Adelaide, South Australia

ISBN 978-0-6481545-0-1

Dulwich Centre Publications
Hutt St PO Box 7192
Adelaide 5000, South Australia
Telephone: +61 (8) 8223 3966
Fax: +61 (8) 8232 4441
Email: dcp@dulwichcentre.com.au
Website: www.dulwichcentre.com.au

To my mum, Erica Denborough,
for living your life with grace,
love, intellect and a belief
in the power of stories.

To Aunty Barbara Wingard
for your wisdom, pride and welcome,
and for so many adventures shared.

Contents

Preface

I grew up with a mother who loves stories. Not only would she read me enchanting stories of fictional worlds, she and I would also create characters and inhabit them in imaginative games. Forty years on, I now witness her doing the same with her grandchildren. My mother's delight in characters, plots, suspense and imagination (and more recently TV drama series!) will live on far beyond her.

It is no coincidence that here I sit, with my fingers on this keyboard, writing a book about practices of story: how to tell stories in ways that bring characters to life; how to travel through story to different worlds and understandings; how stories can transform the everyday into something magical – these are all lessons gifted by my mother.

In my early twenties, it was my great fortune to be embraced by a second 'mother', Aunty Barbara Wingard. I first encountered narrative practice at the time that Dulwich Centre and the Aboriginal Health Council of South Australia were collaborating to respond to Aboriginal families who had lost loved ones due to deaths in custody. Cheryl White introduced me to Kaurna Elder Aunty Barbara Wingard and I began to assist her and Jane Lester as they wrote what was to become the first Aboriginal narrative practice book, *Telling our stories in ways that make us stronger*. Aunty Barbara, Michael White, Cheryl White and I then proceeded to undertake many different adventures.

These adventures were attempts to respond to suffering and injustice. They involved using existing forms of narrative practice and developing new approaches. They involved partnerships across different worlds. They involved both sorrow and laughter. And many of these adventures would begin with the question, 'Do you want to hear a story?'

In contexts of significant hardship, it is sometimes too much to expect people to speak directly about what they are experiencing. Local communities often know that direct speech can be hazardous, can be divisive, can inadvertently make things worse rather than better. And so, when Aunty Barbara would lead us in consultations with a local community that had invited us to visit, she would often begin with, 'Do you want to hear a story? Do you want to hear a story from another community that is also experiencing hard times? They have given us permission to share their experiences with you ...'

Invariably, the sense of relief would be palpable. There would be nods and even a sense of gratitude. Yes, here is a place we can start. Another community has offered us the gift of their stories of sorrow, skills and knowledge. We can listen to their words. Listening is easier than speaking at first.

And then, once the double-storied testimony from another group had been read aloud, Aunty Barbara would ask a further question: 'Would you like to send a message back to them?' And from this vantage point, this place of dignity, a conversation could begin. Words could now flow. New stories could be told and exchanged.

Of course, these are not just any stories being exchanged. These are skilfully crafted double-storied testimonies that convey both the effects of injustices and hardships, and the intricate local knowledge and skills that individuals, families and communities are using to reclaim their lives and futures. Included in this book are many examples of these sorts of testimonies.

Over the last 10 years, as we have explored the possibilities of diverse forms of collective narrative practice, we have grappled with many dilemmas:

- How can our work resist neoliberal fatalism – how can we look for solutions in the right places?

- How can we make our work most relevant to the most marginalised?

- How can we 'democratise' the field by developing methodologies that can be used by concerned community members and/or peers (not only those who have professional training)?

- How can we ensure that our work does not reduce the possibilities for collective local actions? Indeed, how can we create conditions in which local social action is more likely?

In response to these dilemmas and questions, this book offers not answers but stories.

These pages are filled with stories of collective narrative practice projects that have taken place in Australia, Uganda, Palestine, Zimbabwe, Turkey, Kurdistan (Iraq), Thailand, Spain and West Papua. Some of these projects are continuing; others were short-term initiatives. All of them have involved dedicated local practitioners and communities doing all they can to use local knowledge to address injustices, hardships and sorrows.

In the following pages, I also share particular histories in the hope that these provide thinking tools for further creativity and invention. I have drawn upon concepts from diverse writers in order to understand what is taking place as communities exchange rich stories of local skills and initiatives. In doing so, I am seeking to build upon a tradition within the field of narrative therapy and community work that links stories of practice with concepts and ideas drawn from diverse writers and thinkers. This is a tradition linked to:

- Michael White and David Epston, who bequeathed the most exciting ideas and practices that I have ever encountered

- the Just Therapy Team from Aotearoa New Zealand (Flora Tuhaka, Taimalieutu Kiwi Tamasese, Charles Waldegrave and Warihi Campbell) who led the way in living cross-cultural partnerships that are loving, lifelong and intellectually dazzling all at once

- Cheryl White, whose thinking and politics has influenced every project and every page.

As I look over this book, I find myself again thinking of my mum, Erica Denborough, and the parents and caregivers in every community who are preparing children for life through story. I realise now that it was my mum who first enabled me to become enchanted and changed by the stories of others – real or imagined. Gradually, she also introduced me to the creative skills and collaboration required to make up my own stories of life.

These are gifts that keep on giving. They are the basis for all the collective narrative practices described in this book. I hope some of the stories included here may be relevant to your communities. If so, I'd be interested in hearing from you. Perhaps the exchanges can continue.

Acknowledgments

I would like to acknowledge the following practitioners and groups whose work is represented in this book: Ncazelo Ncube-Mlilo; Caleb Wakhungu; IP Kim-ching; Shaista Kalaniya and the young women's groups of the Muslim Women's Association of South Australia; Dr Abdul Stanikzai; Jason McLeod, Tineke Rumkabu, Danny Rayar, Ronny Kareni and others involved in the struggle for West Papuan independence; Anti Macri and Bronwyn McLelland at Adelaide Secondary School of English; Indi Wishart and those involved in the Feast Queer Youth Drop-in Space; Manon van Zuijlen and the International Women's Development Agency; Mònica Florensa, Jordi Freixas and Plataforma d'Afectats per la Hipoteca-Lleida; Mimi Kim, Rachel Herzing and the work of Creative Interventions and The StoryTelling & Organizing Project; Kate Denborough, KAGE Physical Theatre and all those involved in the Team of Life production; and the Jiyang Foundation for Human Rights.

Also included in these pages are profoundly significant contributions from individuals who have chosen for their stories to travel without their names. They have offered their ideas and stories in the hope that their hard-won knowledge, knowledge born out of suffering, will make some difference in the lives of others. Without this determination and generosity, collective narrative practice in general, and the work described in this book, would not be possible. Without this generous, collective ethic, the pages of this book would be blank. Instead, they are filled with stories.

Amaryll Perlesz, David Epston, Cheryl White, Mary Heath, Susanna Chamberlain and David Newman all gave invaluable feedback on earlier drafts. Claire Nettle's editorial acumen significantly enhanced this book.

'Creating "Justice Teams": Unearthing young people's skills in responding to racism' was originally published in *Generation next: Becoming socially enterprising* (Chamberlain, Foxwell-Norton, & Anderson, 2014). It is reprinted with permission of Oxford University Press.

Chapter 6 contains an extended extract from *Raising our heads above the clouds: The use of narrative practices to motivate social action and economic development: The work of Caleb Wakhungu and the Mt Elgon Self-Help Community Project* (Denborough, 2010c). Reprinted with permission of Dulwich Centre Publications.

Chapter 7 contains an extended extract from *Narrative responses to human rights abuses: Sustaining women workers and honouring the survival skills of women from Burma/Myanmar* (Dulwich Centre Foundation International & International Women's Development Agency, 2013). Reprinted with permission of International Women's Development Agency.

The Tree of Life exercise from *Training for transformation* (Hope & Timmel, 1984, p. 38) is reproduced with permission.

All photographs were taken by the author unless otherwise acknowledged.

PART I

SPEAKING THROUGH US, NOT JUST TO US

I was working in Long Bay Prison when I first realised the significance of inviting people to speak through me, not just to me. I can vividly remember the circumstance. I was facilitating a group for men in prison who wished one day to work with young men from their own communities in the hope that their lives wouldn't take the same trajectory as their own. When I mentioned to them that the following week I was going to visit a high school and meet with young men to talk about issues of gender and violence, their eyes lit up. When I asked, 'Shall we make a video message from you all that I could share with them?' there was unanimous agreement.[1]

I still have the videos in which men from diverse cultural backgrounds (but all from contexts of poverty) spoke of how the masculinity they had learnt and taken up had been a 'scholarship to nowhere' (from petty crime to violent crime to prison). They implored young men to refuse such a scholarship. I can also recall how classrooms of unruly teenage boys would suddenly quieten when I mentioned, 'I was at Long Bay Prison last week and the men there made you a video. Would you like to see it?'[2]

I was a young, white, middle-class man (I guess I was about 23 at the time) who had grown up with many privileges. In those moments in the prison and in the classroom I found a different way to use those privileges.[3] I was a member of the 'free world': I didn't hear and feel the closing of the cell door after 'muster' each evening. I had a freedom of movement not available to either the men in prison or the young men in a disadvantaged high school in Sydney's west. These initial exchanges taught me that those of us with privileges, such as freedom of movement, can use these to enable groups that could not otherwise converse to do so. These were not regular conversations. They were exchanges of insider knowledge (Epston, 2014) between collectives in different social locations about particular social issues. They were dignifying, in that both groups experienced making contributions to the other. They were generative of new concepts of life – dominant masculinity as a 'scholarship to nowhere' had never been named in this way before. Significantly, the concepts that were developed and the insider knowledges that were shared explored cracks in the dominant culture (in this case dominant masculinity) and generated counterstories (H. Nelson, 2001).

Twenty-three years later, I remain equally excited at the possibilities of enabling collectives to speak through us, not just to us. In the first chapters of this book, I describe two recent exchanges.

Notes

1. I wonder now how we managed to acquire the necessary permissions, but fortunately the governor of the prison at the time was agreeable to the idea. Deirdre Hyslop was influential in this!

2. For more detailed descriptions of work within Long Bay Prison and work within schools in relation to gender and masculinity, see Denborough (1995a, 1996).

3. The work of the Just Therapy Team, and Charles Waldegrave in particular, has been influential in considering how we can not only acknowledge our privileges, but also use them well. For more about the work of the Just Therapy Team, see Waldegrave, Tamasese, Tuhaka and Campbell (2003).

Chapter 1

Unexpected solidarities:
'We've got to work together'

At present in Australia, many young Muslim women are subject to anti-Islamic hostility and abuse. As part of continuing efforts to highlight contemporary Islamophobia and its effects, and to give voice and agency to those most affected by it, Dulwich Centre Foundation has been involved in a 'life-saving tips' project, which was initiated after the Cronulla Riots.[1] This project involves young Australians of Muslim backgrounds recording tips about dealing with hard times and sharing these with other young people from diverse backgrounds. These initiatives continue to evolve, and more recently we have also begun to focus on supporting the antiracist actions of bystanders (J. Nelson & Dunn, 2011). These initiatives complement each other, because one way to invite bystanders to take action is to publicise the everyday encounters with Islamophobia experienced by Australian Muslims and the diversity of skilful ways in which they are responding to these.

Over the last year, young women from the Muslim Women's Association of South Australia have been interested in sharing with other young people some of the ways in which they are trying not to take people's hate into their hearts. In a series of group discussions, it was my role to ask the occasional question, to 'rescue' (Newman, 2008) the spoken words of young women in writing and to create a draft collective document (Denborough, 2008) which we then revised together. The following document, which they are very happy to have shared with others, was created through this process.

We try not to take people's hate into our hearts[2]

Hi.

We're a group of young Muslim women who live here in Adelaide. We're interested in exchanging ideas and stories about ways of dealing with weird experiences like being stared at, being yelled at by random strangers driving by in their cars, or other strange stuff that happens here and in other places. We've included here some of our stories and the skills we've developed. We'd been keen to hear your ideas!

There are a few different ways that we try not to take people's hate into our hearts.

Keep yourself upright, smile back and remember you are special to someone

I remember when a friend who is Asian came to us one day because she was facing racism at uni. She really cried to us and we were listening. We are black and we wear hijabs. She is not Muslim and has light coloured skin, but we knew that the pain she was experiencing from racism was no different and no less than our own. We started saying to her, if you are going through this, just imagine what we go through each day! Her tears dried and she said, 'How do you do it?' We said you must keep yourself upright and smile back at them. And then I told her my most precious advice: at those times, when facing hostility, remember you are special to someone. This gives you a purpose. You are precious to your family, or to someone you know who loves you. Remember this at those times. Because this gives you a purpose in life, in love. I say to myself, 'I am special to someone. I am going to live for them'. This gives me back my confidence. Otherwise, I could be imagining that people are hating me every single minute. And if you start thinking this, if you start feeling all the time that you are hated, it starts killing you. And you start taking it out on your loved ones. That's why I always try to remember that I am special to someone. I keep myself upright and, to the hostility, I smile back.

Biting back by involving others

When I was a kid, in primary school, if other kids started to give me a hard time, first of all I'd try not to notice it, to brush it off. But if it continued, I'd bite back. I'd take action. It's not okay. I wouldn't do this directly. I would involve others, a third party. If a teacher didn't act, I'd go to my mum.

I still try to do this, to involve others when things are not okay. There was a time recently when I had to go to hospital with my mum. We were sitting in emergency for hours (as you do) and there was this one old man. It always seems to be an old man. He was sitting in the row in front of us. He would turn around to directly face us and just stare. Sometimes staring is worse than saying something because then I can least say something back. When we moved, he would also move. Over time I felt so threatened that I went to the triage desk and asked them to do something. Just to ask him to stop making us feel so uncomfortable. But they said they could not do anything if he was only staring. I don't think that's right. And when things are not right, we need to bite back, and involve others. When we finish this resource, maybe we can take it to all emergency wards.

Replying with humour

Sometimes we find it's better to reply with humour and not take it seriously. I am Muslim but I go to a Christian school here in Adelaide and all sorts of things happen that could make me sad or offended, but instead, I don't take it seriously.

One student kept asking me, 'do you always have to wear a blue scarf?' He thought that Islam only allowed the colour blue, but this was the colour of our school uniform! It seemed he hadn't noticed this. One day we had an excursion where we didn't have to wear a uniform – I wore a rainbow scarf!

In this same school we have to cross ourselves, 'Father, Son and Holy Spirit', all the time! Rather than being sad or offended, I just smile. Everybody is so scared of Muslims at the moment. Humour says we are normal human beings.

My parents are really funny. My dad is a big Arab man with a moustache. He can look very scary to others and sometimes he makes fun of this! I am always saying, 'Dad, you can't do that!' or 'you can't say that'. But he finds himself very funny! And my mum too. I remember when my mother was wearing black, honouring her mother who had passed away. People would say to her, 'Why are you wearing black? You must be very hot. Take off your cardigan'. She would just say, 'Thank you, thank you' and nod as if she couldn't understand English. It was very funny, but I was just shaking my head!

Laughter and friendship

Laughter is also a way of making friends. When I first came to this country it was my dream to make a white friend. There was this one pretty white girl who I really liked. First we shared humour. Then we shared problems. Then we shared our views. Now many years later we have our own beautician business together!

We wish we could control their eyes

Many of us have to deal with people staring at us. When I am crossing a road, there's always one person. And on the train there's one specific man. He sits a few seats away and wears really dark sunglasses. He stares at me for up to 50 minutes. I feel like saying, 'Do you want a picture? It would last longer'. It's especially creepy when it's more than one person staring. I always tell myself, 'I am not doing anything wrong'. I can't control their eyes. Sometimes I wish I could just make them turn away and get on with their own lives. And then I can get on with mine.

Turning hostility into curiosity

When I was about 12, I started wearing the hijab at school, and sometimes other students would ask me hostile questions. I took their questions really seriously, much more seriously than they took them. I always assumed they must genuinely want to know the answer to their question. So if I didn't know the answer, I would look it up. I would go home and ask or read. And then the next day I would find them and tell them the answer. I don't like to be left curious, so I'd always give any hostile question a very full answer. Much fuller than they were ever expecting!

Remembering we have misconceptions too

I find it helpful to remember that we also have misconceptions. When I first came to Australia, I thought we would be riding kangaroos to school. Yes, I was disappointed! And when I saw a big man with tattoos at the airport (he was the quarantine officer) I thought he was so scary. But when he opened his mouth to speak he was so sweet! When people have misconceptions about me I try to remember this. It helps somehow.

These are just some of the ways in which we try not to take people's hate into our hearts. Do you also have ways not to take people's hate into your hearts? If so, we'd love to hear your stories.

It's a richly told account of these young people's diverse skills, isn't it? When I read this document back to them, around a table in the office of the Muslim Women's Association of South Australia, it was as if an informal 'definitional ceremony' (Myerhoff, 1986) were taking place. This was a ceremony that was redefining their identities in each other's eyes. It was also a ceremony of 'political opposition' (Kaminsky, 1993, p. 272) to Islamophobia. These young women had never before heard each other's responses described in these ways. They were unanimous in wanting their document to be shared with other young people, not only because this might assist others who are also facing hatred or hostility, but also because it would raise awareness about Islamophobia, and because this was a document of which they were proud.

An exchange

Not long after this collective document was created, I was invited to visit the Feast Queer Youth Drop-in Space, a regular meeting in a local café. These young people were also receptive to the idea of sharing their life-saving tips with others. It's often a lot easier to recognise and speak about one's own skills of living if you are first able to listen to a resonant story from others. I thought there was a good chance that these young people of diverse sexualities and genders might also know something about 'trying not to take people's hate into their hearts'. So after initial introductions had taken place, I explained a little about what young Muslim women are contending with in public spaces at present and the document they had created, and asked if the young queer folk would be interested in hearing it and responding. They indicated their agreement.

While reading the young Muslim women's words, I was attentive to how they were being received. At first there seemed to be a cautious intrigue, then a poignant recognition. There was occasional joining in laughter. There was also a sense of unexpected solidarity, which is perhaps best conveyed in the stories below that the young queer folk shared as a response to the young Muslim women.

Again, my role was to ask the occasional question (What would you like to say back to the young Muslim women? Why was that story most significant to you? Why do you want to let them know this? How do you want to begin this message? How do you want to sign off?); to 'rescue' their spoken words in writing; and to incrementally read back the message that was being created through our conversation.

Through this process, the following message was developed.

G'day.

Tonight at the Feast Queer Youth Drop-in Space, we heard some of the ways you try not to take people's hate into your hearts. Thanks for sharing your stories with us.

One of us smiled when we heard you had expected to be riding kangaroos to school in Australia ☺. I thought that too! I came from England and had all these misconceptions about Australia. Apart from riding kangaroos, I thought it would be hot all year round. I was worried about drop bears and I thought Vegemite was something you put in your drink!

We were all really sorry to hear about what you sometimes have to face with people staring or shouting abuse.

Some of us also have to deal with abusive comments, or misunderstanding and rejection, or even harassment and violence because of homophobia or transphobia. So it was good to hear how you deal with things.

I found your first idea really quite beautiful: 'Keep yourself upright, smile back and remember you are special to someone'. I'd like to add something to that.

It's important to me to remember that there are people who love me, and it's also important for me to love myself, to be kind to myself. To hold myself with pride. To take pride in even little things that we do. This is not about being selfish. This is about being self-caring. It took me years to learn that there is value in caring for yourself. Being selfish is when you put your wants over the needs of others. But when you put your needs over the wants of others, that's not selfish, that's self-preservation. We've had to learn about this.

We also really liked hearing the story of how one of you wore a rainbow scarf on your school excursion to show to the boy who thought you could only wear blue! We laughed out loud when we heard this. It might not surprise you that here at the Feast Drop-in there are plenty of rainbows. One of us is even wearing long rainbow stockings!

We have a few other ways that we also use to not take hate into our hearts.

'Sorry, I don't understand that'

Homophobia is often conveyed as if it is a joke. I've found it works quite well if I simply say in a thoughtful, curious voice, 'Sorry, I don't understand that, I don't understand the joke, can you explain it to me?' Often the person then finds it very hard to answer. In fact, once they start to try to explain what they have said, they feel awkward or uncomfortable. The awkwardness somehow bounces off me and goes back to them. Hopefully this will mean they won't say it next time.

Using my size (or lack of it)

I'm the size of a 10-year-old. Occasionally, if someone is being a bully, I have stood in their way, in between them and the person they are hurting. I've found that when someone the size of a 10-year-old girl stands in the way, then they generally only throw words, not punches. I think this is because they feel it would be taking their power too far otherwise. There are times when someone has to get in there, stand up and be like a wall. So occasionally I use my size – or lack of it!

What of it?

Often 'gay' is used as an insult. If someone uses it that way to me, and says, 'You're gay', I simply say, 'Yeah, I'm gay, what of it? I'm also wearing shoes today'. Or 'I'm also A-positive blood type'. This is about acknowledging truth. But it's also about contentment. They offer an insult to me. I offer back acknowledgment and contentment.

We were so sorry to hear about the horrible things that happen for you guys at bus stops, and in buses and trains.

One of us wanted to share a story back with you.

Back in January, I was gay bashed on a train. They were only 15 years old. It was pretty frightening. I couldn't face going back on a train for about a month. But then I did. How did I get the strength to go back again? I guess I've had to be really strong for a long time. As a Jewish gay boy, back at school I was gay bashed and anti-Semitic bashed. I guess I developed some sort of resistance. It had to be a smart resistance. I think you've always got to respond, but in an intelligent way, in a smart way.

They were actually harassing a girl before me. She was sitting near me and they were being really sexist. They were being pigs. I was kind of sorry I hadn't done anything earlier, but then they targeted me. I was trying to hold them off with words, but it was getting pretty scary, and I said they had to stop this or I would call the police. It was actually when I was calling the police that they decided to hit me and then ran for it. There were security cameras rolling, the police were already on the way, and when they searched the area they found them. I was glad I was smart enough not to physically hit back. I learnt at school that whenever I was violent back to defend myself I'd always end up on detention as well.

So this time round, I used a smart resistance. To be honest, they weren't that smart and they've now been charged. They have to face their own parents and me. The court case is still playing on. I really wouldn't want them to go to juvenile detention. They are only 15. I know they will regret it when they are older. And it's not about blaming the parents either. You can't control what a 15-year-old does. There is this good youth justice program where offenders sit down with victims, and I just want them to learn. I've seen a lot of people change, like the boys who beat me up at school. I recently met up with those same guys at uni. They are doing really well now. Doing interesting things. And they apologised to me. I can see they really regret what they did. So I know these 15-year-olds are going to regret this one day. They're going to have to live with that regret.

I learnt a lot back in high school. It was a Catholic school, but it had a lot of Muslim students and me, a Jewish student. The Muslim students were the main instigators of the anti-Semitism, but I never let this get the better of me. I knew it was mostly to do with the politics of the Middle East and I don't agree with everything Israel is doing, just as I know you wouldn't agree with terrorism. The anti-Semitism at school never made me see Muslim people in a particular way. I had a close Muslim friend who was questioning his sexuality. We may have kissed a couple of times. But it was never going to go anywhere. When I changed schools, my best friend was a Muslim girl from Sudan. We would walk down Rundle Mall together. She would cop a lot of racist comments and I was always defending her.

I am scared about the rise of Islamophobia in Australia and the parallels we can draw with anti-Semitism in the 1930s in Germany. What happened to my people then is what is happening to your people now. I know it's only a minority of Australians who are Islamophobic, but they are loud so it feels like the majority and it is scary.

You know when people say we don't want the actions of terrorists to change our lives? I don't want the Islamophobic people to change our lives either. And I didn't want to live in fear after the gay bashing, so it was important for me to start taking the train again.

There are lots of connections between racism and homophobia. History tells us they are companions. *PPl. who experience both ...*

It was really good to hear your ideas. We've got to work together.

A second exchange

When we next met at the Muslim Women's Association, I brought with me three different messages in response to the young women's document, 'We try not to take people's hate into our hearts'. These were from teachers, from a group of young Afghanis and the above message from the Feast Queer Youth Drop-in Space.

Reading these messages back to the young Muslim women created a second definitional ceremony. There was a resounding quietness as I read. When I asked the young Muslim women if they would like to send a response to the young Jewish man, this is what they said:

> It was so interesting to hear this story from this young man. His heart is so beautiful.
>
> He made so many connections.
>
> It was good to hear his train story.
>
> And how he didn't make the same mistakes he made at high school. He found a way to respond without fighting back. We really respect that.
>
> I think it would be good for other young men to hear his story. About how he did that. It's a story of preventing violence. It'd be good for other young men to hear it.
>
> It is a really smart story. He doesn't want the boys to go to juvenile prison. He wants them to learn. He wants them to change.
>
> And it's a strong story – the way he went back with strength. He is riding trains again now.
>
> Yes, and brave too. Despite going through the problems at school, when he was on the train, he still wanted to help the young woman.
>
> Please send a message back to him from us. Please thank him for sharing his smart, strong, brave story with us.
>
> He made so many connections. His heart is so beautiful.

Counterstories

I am continually moved by what becomes possible when people are invited to speak through us, not just to us. I found this exchange particularly moving. Why? At this time in Australia and beyond there is a rise in 'hate speech': Islamophobia, racism, anti-Semitism, homophobia and transphobia. I am not sure what the opposite of hate speech is, but I suspect this exchange might just be an example. If hate speech generates and sustains division and bigotry, this sort of exchange creates a counterstory.

Hilde Lindemann Nelson (2001), a feminist ethicist and philosopher, has written in detail about counterstories in relation to group identity, focusing on situations in which there is a clear oppressor/oppressed relationship. What is relevant about Nelson's descriptions and examples of master stories and counterstories is that they are not restricted to narratives of relationship between individuals. Instead, she considers broader cultural stories and discourses about collective identities, such as women, transgender folk, Roma people. Nelson maps the 'master narratives' that influence how individuals and groups understand themselves and others, and the ways in which counterstories are developed in resistance:

Counterstories come into being through a process of ongoing engagement with the narratives they resist. Many of them start small, like a seed in the crack of a sidewalk, but they are capable of displacing surprising chunks of concrete as they grow.

How much of the sidewalk a counterstory displaces is a function of the degree to which it resists the master narrative. Because the purpose of a counterstory is to repair an identity, the resistance it offers must, at a minimum, aim to dislodge some portion of the master narrative from a person's understanding of who she herself is, even if there is no attempt to push the counterstory into the broader community. (H. Nelson, 2001, p. 169)

Nelson also proposes certain characteristics of 'good' or 'successful' counterstories:

Good counterstories aim to free not only individuals but the entire group whose identity is damaged by an oppressive master narrative. They don't try to free one group by oppressing another, nor do they throw out moral understandings that ought to be left in place. They are credible because they offer the best available explanation of who the group members are, they correlate strongly with the group members' actions, and they weigh the various characteristics of the group accurately, so that the representation of the group members is a faithful one. (H. Nelson, 2001, pp. 183–184)

In times of increasing division, creating the conditions for the generation and circulation of counterstories is one possible response.[3]

'Third voice' exchanges

One way of understanding the ways in which these documents are written is through Barbara Meyerhoff's concept of the 'third voice', 'which is neither the voice of the informant nor the voice of the interviewer, but the voice of their collaboration' (Myerhoff, quoted in Kaminsky, 1992b, p. 127). Myerhoff 'wished to find a way of editing the personal narratives that she had collected, so that everything she know about them would be invisibly embedded in the tale, through the editing' (Kaminsky, 1992b, p. 128).

'We try not to take people's hate into our hearts' and the response from the young queer folk, were shaped by the questions I asked and the responses I offered as interviewer. These questions and comments are invisibly embedded or implicit in the text, but they are not transparent. There are complexities involved in this, and processes of accountability and feedback are critical. In addition to reading drafts and asking for feedback and changes, longstanding relationships with Shaista Kalaniya and the Muslim Women's Association of South Australia meant that I was confident that if any of the young Muslim women were not happy with any aspects of their document that they could speak with Shaista and she would speak with me. Indeed, changes have been made to the document and will continue to be made to it.[4] Similarly, the response from the queer youth was shared first, via email, with the young man whose individual story is told within it. The draft was then read to the group before there was agreement for it to be shared with the young Muslims. The draft was also shared with the facilitator of the youth group, Indi Wishart, for further feedback. Perhaps these processes can be conceived as efforts towards creating an 'accountable third voice' and a 'genuinely dialogical text' (Kaminsky, 1992b, p. 130).

Even with such considerations of accountability, however, there are times when third voice documentation is not appropriate. In some circumstances, it seems vitally important to preserve individual voices (in their distinct cultural vernacular) and also to make clearly visible the distinction between the voice of interviewee and interviewer.[5]

What can these exchanges make possible?

The sort of exchange described in this chapter is obviously not going to end Islamophobic or homophobic attacks. These exchanges do, however, enable groups that could not otherwise converse to do so.

Can these ways of working, at the very least, support 'everyday forms of resistance' (Scott, 1990, p. 8)? Could they make more possible the conditions for diverse groups marginalised by the dominant culture to not only converse, but also collaborate? Could they create opportunities for unexpected solidarities? The words of the young Jewish gay man in response to the young Muslim women ring in my ears: 'We've got to work together'.

What's more, perhaps these processes can catalyse action from members of dominant groups. We are now convening forums in which 'We try not to take people's hate into our hearts' is witnessed by non-Muslim Australians in order to raise consciousness about Islamophobia and to spark bystanders into action. We will then document actions taken by non-Muslim bystanders to address Islamophobia and circulate these.[6]

The possibilities for enabling people to speak through us, not just to us, seem limitless. In a quite different context, one of the most significant and rigorous exchanges of this kind was convened between Aboriginal communities to support each other in relation to grief and to provide young people with reasons to live (see Denborough, Koolmatrie, Mununggirritj, Marika, Dhurrkay & Yunupingu, 2006). And in the next chapter, I describe a process in which young Syrians who have recently come to Australia as refugees are making lives in a new land and exchanging stories, skills and knowledge at the same time.

I wish to end this chapter, however, on a note of caution. Care needs to be taken to ensure that any such exchange does not reify identities based on only one theme. As Amartya Sen eloquently describes, 'identities are robustly plural' (2006, p. 19). In our work we must be cautious not to reify 'singular affiliations' (Sen, 2006, p. 20). Those involved in the exchanges described in this chapter have multiple and diverse affiliations and associations of identity. It is my hope that exchanges such as those described here can play a part in diffusing or multiplying storylines of identity.[7]

Notes

1. The initial life-saving tips project was created in the aftermath of the Cronulla Riots (see www.sbs.com.au/cronullariots/). It was one of many initiatives taken in the hope of diminishing racism and anti-Muslim sentiment in this country. Because the Cronulla Riots took place at the beach, we decided to use the metaphor of 'life-saving' to describe the sharing of tips between diverse groups of young Australians. To view the resources from this project, see www.dulwichcentre.com. au/projects/life-saving-tips/

2. A video version of this document can be viewed at: www.dulwichcentre.com.au/ encyclopedia

3. As mentioned, we are also in the midst of supporting and encouraging action from 'bystanders' and people with privilege taking action to address hate. Ensuring that the responsibility for responding to hate is not left with those most affected by it seems a critical principle.

4. One change to the document was made when a young woman asked to include the phrase 'we knew that the pain she was experiencing from racism was no different or no less than our own'. A second change was to move the theme 'Biting back by involving others' up towards the beginning of the document. This occurred after the document was read to a group of newly arrived Syrian mothers (see Chapter 2) and they spoke passionately about how racism must be responded to with action.

5. For an example, see 'We were suffering for our kids: This is how we got them back', an interview with Adam Martin (Wingard & Dulwich Centre Foundation, 2015).

6. For more information, see www.dulwichcentre.com.au/bystander

7. We must also take care to ensure that identities such as 'young Muslim' or 'young LGBTQ+ folks' are never spoken of in ways that imply they are mutually exclusive.

Chapter 2

Making lives in a new land:
Young Syrians writing / speaking
to each other across time and place

And all the countries seemed the same
That I don't see myself there
And I don't see myself here

– Nizar Qabbani

The one thing I love most about sleeping the night
is it makes me forget the day's bombing. Bana #Aleppo
(Tweet from 7-year-old Bana Alabed, 20 November 2016)

Adelaide is a long way from Aleppo. This chapter describes a project that took place in Adelaide while Aleppo was under siege and Syria was in the midst of civil war. It includes collective letters written by and with young Syrians who, with their families, had recently arrived in Australia as refugees.

Invitations

Shortly after a number of Syrian families arrived as refugees in Adelaide, I received an email from Bronywn McClelland, a colleague at Adelaide Secondary School of English. This vibrant school provides a vital pathway for students who have had severely disrupted schooling and who arrive in Australia without being able to speak English. She wrote:

Hi David,

We are currently responding to a very large influx of around 60 students from Syria (mostly via Jordan). We are finding that they are (understandably) generally hyper-aroused, hyper-vigilant, and, as they gain more language to tell us, more and more bits of what they have lived through over the past few years are emerging. It has obviously had a huge impact on them.

There have been some difficulties. For example, a disagreement between one Afghani boy and one Syrian boy over something that was said to a girl exploded into a very tense stand-off between large groups of students from the two cultures, and there has also been some conflict in the city after school. In addition to the inter-student conflict, the teachers involved in working closely with these students are finding it a definite challenge.

As a school, we are trying to put as much support as we can in place for these newly arrived students, and to be proactive in terms of addressing their wellbeing needs as a matter of priority – knowing that unless this is addressed, it will be difficult for the students to settle and learn. We are also learning as much as we can about the contexts from which these students have come – we are screening a documentary about the camps in Jordan, and a few members of the Syrian community are coming to speak with us in a few weeks' time.

We are wondering about whether there might be a possibility of someone from your centre, or who you know of, doing some work with four classes of prominently Syrian students to help them and us?

In a phone conversation with Bronwyn and deputy principal Anti Macri, I learnt more about what the Syrian students had shown interest in (football and song) and also that there had been two Syrian brothers who had arrived earlier in Adelaide and who had now 'graduated' and moved into a mainstream Adelaide high school.

I have no idea what it is like to move country as a young person: to arrive in a new landscape not speaking the language; to have lost connection with dear friends; to know that your loved ones are still in danger. I have no idea what it takes to make a new life in a different land. I thought, however, that the two brothers who had arrived six months earlier, and who had passed through the same school, may well have vital knowledge to share.

In a quick email exchange with Yazan, the older brother, I found that they were very interested in sharing what they had learnt about making a new life. As it happened, we met up on Eid al-Adha, one of the most holy days in the Muslim calendar. The three of us sat around my table at Dulwich Centre. With permission, I took notes as we spoke, and that evening I drafted their words into the following collective letter.

To the Syrian students at Adelaide Secondary School of English

Hi.

We are two Syrian brothers. We arrived as refugees in Adelaide in December last year – not so long ago. We are happy to share our stories of how we are trying to make a new life here in Adelaide.

Today is Eid al-Adha. The whole celebration of Eid is about making some sacrifice and providing for people who are in need. Now we are living in Adelaide so we are not able to visit our family members who are still in Syria or in the camps. We miss this. When you visit your family members it makes you feel happy and it feels like a real Eid celebration.

We are from Aleppo, one of the oldest cities in the world. There is a castle there built about 10 000 years ago. It's a city of many cultures and a city of many different languages, very old languages.

Because it is such an important city, it has been most damaged in the war. Our uncle and grandfather are still there in Aleppo. They don't have electricity or connection all the time so it is hard to call them. We worry about them and try to call. We ask if they have enough food for everyone – can they get enough water, is everyone okay?

It is very hard when we see on TV that there has been an explosion. We rush to call them, to check that everyone is alright. But the networks will be down and we are afraid until they get a network again and can call us to tell us they are okay.

We all feel the same at those times. All of us Syrians who are far from home. We all feel sorry. No-one wants the war to happen.

We tell our families there is a hope that everything will be alright one day. That is all we can do: have hope.

And make the most of our chance here for a new life.

When we first arrived in Adelaide, we realised this is a very quiet city. In the Middle East there is much more noise and life in the nights. Here it is so quiet! And we got lost so many times. We had to use Google Maps a lot! I remember when my phone battery suddenly stopped working so no more Google Maps. Luckily we were together as brothers so I could use my brother's phone to get home.

After the first couple of months, we started to know about our suburb, and then how to use the bus to go to the city, and then how to go to our school by ourselves.

Our first school was Adelaide Secondary School of English. It was a really good school. But, actually I wanted to get out from that school as quickly as possible because it was so far away from my home – one hour and a half in the bus each way! From my first day in that school, I decided that I didn't want to spend three hours in the bus coming to school and going back to home, so I decided to learn English as quickly as possible.

So I forced myself to make friendships with people from other cultures and not just talk to others in Arabic.

In my first term there were just 10 students in the whole school who could speak Arabic. I didn't try to make friendships with them. If I had made friendships only with people who speak my language, I'm sure I'd have needed to stay there, in that school, for more than five months.

The first friend I made was Ryan. He's from Vietnam. I like soccer and I always saw him playing soccer with his friends during lunchtime in the school. One time I asked if I could join him, and he didn't mind. We started playing and he was in most of my classes. We became friends and we had to talk to each other in English.

My younger brother's first friend was from Afghanistan. They became friends because they both like playing chess. They met in the library.

At first we used very simple language to talk with our new friends, but we kept practicing. Mostly we talked about soccer. We were from different countries, different cultures, different languages, but we had the same interest – soccer. That's what was important. Then I added Ryan on Facebook so I could chat with him after school.

The other thing that really helped me learn English was watching action movies on TV. I always used to watch movies in English with subtitles, but here I forced myself to watch without subtitles. Action movies in English, without subtitles, have helped me.

Spending time at Marion shopping centre was good too. In our first couple of months we didn't know any other Syrian families here. We didn't know anyone at all. So instead of staying at home all the time, I tried to go to Marion. And to the library sometimes. I'd speak to people working in the shops. That's how I'd practice my English, just asking about things.

These were the first steps we had to take in making a new life here – finding our way (not getting so lost!), making friendships through soccer and chess, and learning the language.

It was also good to discover some beautiful places, like Adelaide Oval and the river, especially at night, the beautiful lights. And Mt Lofty. We went on a camping excursion there and got to know the land. There are a lot of beautiful colours there. Glenelg, the beach is really nice.

In our family, we had to keep encouraging each other. Older brothers take the harder work and most of the responsibility. My father is a completely new English learner. He is studying now and sometimes he struggles with his homework so I try to explain things for him. He speaks Arabic and French and he is teaching my younger brother French. Finding other Arabic speakers was very good for my mother. And spending time together was important. In our first house we didn't have internet connection, we had to use mobile data, and this actually made us spend more time with each other. It turned out to be a good thing. After a while, my mum, my dad and my brother, we all started to volunteer to help new arrivals. To meet people at the airport. It was good doing this together.

But it was really hard for us at first. Even time is different here. Australians are very accurate about times. But in Syria, a lot of people, they don't go to the places at the exact time or accurate time. We kept saying to ourselves, we know that it's completely different here to where we came from so we need to adapt. This is not optional. Many things were a big struggle.

What kept us going? It was a passion. A passion to be part of this new community. And to help others when they first arrive.

Most of you who have just arrived have come from Lebanon or Jordan or Turkey. You've come from the camps where you didn't go to school for three or four years. I know that some of you had to work because the governments there don't provide money for Syrian refugees to go to school. And in the winter, in the camps, it's a really hard life. We think you have a passion too. You had a passion to stay alive.

We are two Syrian brothers. We're from Aleppo. A city of many cultures and many different languages.

Soon I will go into year 11. I am going to study 3D designing, sound production, photography and graphic design. I'm interested in programming too. I've already been in a few competitions. My younger brother wants to be a neurologist. But he's only in year 8.

This is our story of how we're making a new life here in Adelaide. Thank you for listening to us. We'd like to hear your stories.

About this letter

This letter is created in what anthropologist Barbara Myerhoff (in Kaminsky, 1992b) referred to as the 'third voice'. The questions that I asked during our conversation do not appear in the text, but they were influential in its creation. The letter represents the knowledge that was generated from our collaboration. I felt free to edit the brothers' spoken words into this written form because I shared the draft with Yazan and his brother, and checked they were happy with its form and content before it was shared with anyone else.

I had no idea what would emerge in our conversation. As it turned out, the conversation lingered around a number of key themes:

- the meaning of Eid al-Adha and the experience of this in a new country
- an honouring of the city of Aleppo
- how, as young people, these brothers were responding to the continuing crises and concerns for loved ones in Aleppo.

As the brothers' responses were explored and documented, a particularly significant passage emerged:

We all feel the same at those times. All of us Syrians who are far from home. We all feel sorry. No-one wants the war to happen.

We tell our families there is a hope that everything will be alright one day. That is all we can do: have hope.

And make the most of our chance here for a new life.

As I heard these words, it was clear they were being spoken not only individually, but collectively: that young Syrian refugees are carrying sorrow, hope and a responsibility to make the most of a new chance at life, all at once.

I was surprised at some of the other key themes:

- the vivid descriptions of disorientation and getting lost so often in a new city
- tips about how to learn English more quickly
- special knowledge about how to make friends in a new country
- the significance of making connections with beautiful places in a new homeland
- sparkling and ambitious hopes for their personal futures.

Importantly, this is a double-storied letter. It includes rich acknowledgments of the hardships faced by loved ones in Syria and by newcomers to Australia – profound worries about relatives still in zones of war; the experience of being in refugee camps in Jordan or Turkey; getting hopelessly lost in a new city; the struggles of fathers who are totally new at English; the profoundly disconcerting quietness of Adelaide nights. The way these acknowledgments were woven throughout the conversation and text enabled the emergence of a second storyline: a storyline that depicts the skills, responses and knowledge of these two Syrian brothers (and simultaneously, young Syrian refugees more collectively). The second storyline within this letter acknowledges skills in learning a new language, forming new friendships and living life with a passion 'to help others when they first arrive'. As it happened, the invitation to create this letter to assist new arrivals was profoundly resonant with this passion and further enabled its expression.

The two brothers were speaking not just to me, but through me to the newly arrived Syrian students. This was the reason for our meeting. This was why I felt free to ask the questions that I did: we were joined in a broader purpose.

There was so much I did not know about the experience of the newly arrived students at Adelaide Secondary School of English. I was confident, however, that something about the themes of the brothers' letter would resonate with them. I hoped that both storylines of the letter would be significant. The descriptions of hardships might generate a sense of acknowledgment from young people to young people. The descriptions of skills and tips and hopes for the future might offer a glimpse of how such hardships could be endured and transformed.

'Thank you for writing to us'

When I arrived at the school to share the letter with the students, I learnt that Anti Macri had come up with terrific idea. She had asked for representatives of each of the Syrian classes to come together to hear the letter and then share the news and stories of the process with each of their classes.

A translator was present as I read aloud the words of Yazan and his brother. When I mentioned that the letter was from brothers from Aleppo, two students indicated that they were also from Aleppo. The energy in the room changed as the letter was shared. Occasionally there was laughter as students recognised themselves in the brothers' accounts of getting lost and finding that even time was different in Australia. There was focus when hearing the stories of how they sought to learn English and re-make their lives. And there was poignancy in the room with every acknowledgment of hardship.

After I had shared the letter, I asked the students if they would like to write a response. I offered to take notes and a collective process ensued. Different students offered ideas of what to convey back to the brothers. The following letter emerged.

To the two Syrian brothers from Aleppo

Thank you for writing to us!

We are a group of 20 Syrian students here at Adelaide Secondary School of English. We listened to your letter this morning and it was very interesting to us. We have all had some similar experiences to you! Two of us are from Aleppo like you.

When we first arrived here, we had feelings of loneliness. Some of us stayed in our houses a lot. Some of us were very isolated, even crying and weeping. We felt so far away from home.

We agree with you that all aspects of life are SO different here. The way people communicate, even the way people share feelings is different.

When you talked about getting lost, many of us nodded and agreed. We have got lost a lot too. All the housing here looks the same. It is so easy to get lost.

When we first arrived we also seemed to have so many appointments with doctors, more and more appointments, but now we are starting to settle in.

And here it is safe and secure. Before, we had a very different life. For people back in Syria, or in the camps, now is a time of war, massacres and carnage.

One of us, who spent years in the refugee camps in Jordan before coming to this school, said, 'We feel here at this school that we are safe and secure. This school has become home. We are happy to be with our friends here'.

Another one of us said, 'I liked hearing how you made friends with students of other cultures, how you started to talk with others. When I first arrived, I was very attached to the Syrian community; now I am capable of communicating with everyone'.

We also agree that we need to encourage each other in our families. We help our parents especially with how to speak English. We are learning together. This is our life. We have faced many hardships, and still are, but we have to encourage each other, like how you have encouraged us. Now we will share your story with each of our classes.

Thank you for your letter. Your words lifted us up a little bit. Your story gives us hope that we will have a better future.

From your friends at Adelaide Secondary School of English.

About this letter: Speaking from friendship, looking back and looking forward

There would have been no reason for these young people to speak with me, or any of the teachers at the school, about some of the themes they touch upon in this letter. The reason they spoke was because they were replying to the other young Syrians who had kindly written to them. There was a reason for them to speak. Their words were spoken and written in friendship.

There was, I think, something significant about how this letter positioned the students in time. It enabled them to look both forward and backward in particular ways. The fact that the two brothers had only arrived in Adelaide six months previously, and yet had clearly learnt so much in those six months, enabled the newly arrived students to look forward and consider where they might be in six months' time. I believe that this was a key factor in why they said:

Thank you for your letter. Your words lifted us up a little bit. Your story gives us hope that we will have a better future.

Interestingly, because in their letter the two brothers were looking back at their initial experiences in Adelaide, this gave the newly arrived students a way to look backward on their first weeks in Australia:

When we first arrived here we had feelings of loneliness. Some of us stayed in our houses a lot. Some of us were very isolated, even crying and weeping. We felt so far away from home.

This enabled an acknowledgment of sorrows that I have no doubt many of the newly arrived students were still experiencing. This was a communalisation of sorrows, a performance of 'communitas'[1] in relation to isolation, and in some ways this can play a part in altering one's relationship to it. Significantly, this process also made it possible for these experiences of profound loneliness and isolation to be placed differently in time. They were now linked to a theme of 'When we first arrived here'. Implicit in this phrase is 'We are now further along' or 'in a different territory'. While this may not necessarily reduce the influence of isolation and sorrow, it does somehow alter their rhythm or their placement in time.

Hannah Arendt (1943/1994) wrote evocatively about the experience of exile:

We lost our home, which means the familiarity of daily life. We lost our occupation, which means the confidence that we are of some use in the world. We lost our language, which means the naturalness of reactions, the simplicity of gestures, the unaffected expression of feelings. We left relatives in the Polish ghettos and our best friends have been killed in concentration camps, and that means the rupture of our private lives. (Arendt, 1943/1994, p. 110)

In these first two letters between young Syrians, they also articulated their experiences of an altered experience of time ('Even time is different here') and ways of sharing feelings ('The way people communicate, even the way people share feelings is different'). The process of writing/ speaking to each other in these ways generated a vocabulary to describe the young people's experience of exile, and of making a new life within a vastly different cultural landscape.

Writing back

As it happened, I was soon to be travelling with colleagues from Dulwich Centre Foundation to Turkey.[2] I knew that on this trip we would be travelling close to the Syrian border and that there would be opportunities to meet with young Syrians who were seeking safety in Turkey. As many of the newly arrived students had only recently been living in communities and/or camps in Jordan or Turkey, I thought that they might be interested in corresponding in some way with young people in similar situations to those they had recently faced.

I didn't know exactly what would come of such an exchange, but I thought it might enable the newly arrived students to articulate some of the ways in which they had endured their time in Jordan and Turkey. As Nihaya Abu-Rayyan (2014) explained, utilising a rites of passage metaphor and richly describing the skills used in enduring hardship in earlier seasons of life can make visible more options for action in the present:

In all of our lives, we move through different rites of passage; for instance from being a child to an adult. As we live life on one stage, we face particular changes and challenges and we develop our own expertise. All that we learn on one stage of life affects who we are and how we relate to those we know. When the time comes to separate from one way of living and to move to another, these are moments of enormous challenge. Everything that is familiar and comfortable on the first stage is no longer. We are forced to face changes and new struggles. Life doesn't always provide us with choices. Sometimes we are placed in situations beyond our control and it is then that we must find ways to live and to protect our sense of self from being demolished.

When we move from one stage of life to another, it can make all the difference if we use the expertise we developed on the first stage in order to face the difficult situations of the next. All that we learnt in autumn can assist us to deal with winter. All that we learnt during winter can help us throughout spring. And all that we learnt in spring can provide comfort during summer, and so on. Only when there is this sense of continuity can we look forward to life. And as the seasons cycle, we can then remember what we have passed through, how we have changed, and how we have remained the same. (Abu-Rayyan, 2014, p. 28)

This is the letter that emerged from a group conversation with the newly arrived students:

To young Syrians in Turkey

We are a group of Syrian young people who have recently arrived in Australia as refugees. Some of us came from Turkey, some from camps in Jordan.

When I was in the camps, sometimes I felt utterly hopeless. There was so much boredom, monotony and despair. I had no chance to go to school there.

If you are living in camps, we all wish you will get out very soon. That you can go back home, if everything has calmed down, or that you can come here to Australia – or somewhere else safe.

If you do come to Australia, at first it can be a bit hard. When we first came here we felt lonely and a bit hopeless. It is so different here. But we realise we are like the pioneers of the Syrian refugees. We are working for opportunities and to study. We are going to build a new life here and be a guide to those coming after us. We will be here to welcome you. We are waiting for you.

As we wrote this letter to you, some of us had sparkling eyes. Even though we are talking about serious things, we also try to joke together. We have learnt that this is important.

As refugees, there is a lot of waiting, boredom, monotony and despair. We try to support each other, joke with each other to keep our spirits up. Some of us use the internet and soap operas for this whenever we can. Some of us like soccer.

What do you do to deal with the boredom? What do you do to encourage each other?

We hope to hear from you.

We are waiting for you.
Your friends in Adelaide, Australia.

About this letter: creating a usable past

The creation of this letter had three distinct phases. In the first, an older young man, who had been one of the young people to openly state he had spent some years in a refugee camp in Jordan, spoke eloquently about his experience of monotony and hopelessness. This was a young man who had spent years out of schooling and so coming to an Australian school where he was needing to learn a new language, English, had posed significant challenges. I was delighted that this process enabled him to speak on behalf of the collective.

The second significant moment was when younger members of the group spoke of the loneliness that newcomers might experience if they make it Australia, but then pivoted to a different speaking position:

'we realise we are like the pioneers of the Syrian refugees. We are working for opportunities and to study. We are going to build a new life here and be a guide to those coming after us. We will be here to welcome you. We are waiting for you.'

In this moment, their past, recent and present experiences of hardship took on a different meaning. Time shifted slightly as a 'usable past' (Wertsch, 2002, p. 45) was created. The difficulties of their experience were now available for them to use to welcome others – the people they were addressing, whom they were now waiting for.

The third shift occurred non-verbally. After they had spoken of being here to welcome others, there were a number of cheeky, sparkling interactions between the young people. It was a chance for me to acknowledge this and to say, 'it seems like even though we are talking about serious things, you also try to joke together? Is this important?' And so began a brief but significant conversation about some of their ways of dealing with 'waiting, boredom, monotony and despair'. I was given a quick education about Arabic soap operas and we thought it would be a good idea to ask the young people in Turkey about some of their ways of encouraging each other.

I read back the notes I had taken for their letter to the two Syrian brothers and to the young people in Turkey. They recognised the words I had 'rescued' and there was a sense of pride and appreciation in their eyes. I thanked them for their letters. I told them I would pass them on and that I'd be back when I had responses for them.

A response from close to the Syrian Border

During our time in Turkey, we visited Kilis, a Turkish city close to the Syrian border that had received over 120 000 refugees, which meant the number of refugees in Kilis exceeded the number of local residents.[3] While there, we met with a number of young Syrian psychologists who had themselves fled to Turkey and were now working with other Syrian families. We read them the letter from the students in Adelaide, and with their permission rescued their words and shaped them in to this response:

Hello from the House of the Lemon Tree
Kilis, Turkey, close to the Syrian border

Dear friends in Adelaide,

Figure 1. The House of the Lemon Tree, Kilis, Turkey

Today we received your letter.

After we heard it, one of us said, 'This letter has given me energy for a month!' Thank you for thinking of us.

We are from Syria but are living in Kilis in Turkey, close to the border. We work in a place called the House of the Lemon Tree. Here is a picture.

We are trying to bring hope to Syrian families here. We visit people in their homes and they welcome us. We show that there is someone who cares for them. We drink coffee together.

Or sometimes we go to the garden. Sometimes it makes a difference to have company, especially for people who have been afraid to leave the house.

We have lived the same things as the people we meet with.

And earlier this year, there were bombings here in Kilis. Sometimes it can be very hard.

In your letter you asked, 'What do you do to encourage each other?' It's different for each of us:

- 'Talking with each other is important. Whenever I need to, I turn to my friend and talk with her. She has a way of making me feel better each time.'

- 'For me, I have a philosophy. I believe in goodness. I believe that the people who are causing destruction don't know what they are doing.'

- 'I try to bring a touch of life to others. To share a smile with a child and for them to smile back. When we make that connection that is what keeps me going.'

- 'I am doing this to help people and there is meaning in this. Each day I know I am doing this for something. And this helps me.'

- 'It's different for all of us but we all want a better world.'

We are also trying to make connections between people, to make links, so that we can all help one another. And today we received your letter from the other side of the world. After we heard it, one of us said, 'This letter has given me energy for a month!'

Thank you!

A different kind of travelling

When I returned to Adelaide Secondary School of English, one of the young people immediately asked, 'Do you have a response for us?' As I read the letter from Kilis, there was a sense of reverence for the words of those close to the Syrian border. There was a sense of intrigue as to the philosophies that were articulated in the letter, and it seemed to me there was sense of accomplishment when they learnt that their letter had supplied 'energy for a month' to people reaching out to suffering families. As I read the letter, I passed around photographs from Kilis, and the students took turns to peer at them.

In an interview (Said & Marranca, 1991), Edward Said spoke with Marc Robinson about the experience of exile as being a 'kind of traffic' between the past, an ideal future and a dangerous, equivocal present:

Robinson: It's also very much in the nature of the exile. I mean, there's a sense that you're either living in the past or living in an ideal future, and the present is such a dangerous equivocal realm where you can't place yourself, and yet you're forced to. . . .

Said: . . . I don't think there's a formula for it. I think one can call it a kind of traffic between those situations. (Said & Marranca, 1991, pp. 27–28)

This exchange of collective letters enabled the young people in Adelaide to travel/traffic between their past, future and present in particular ways. Only months ago, the young students had been in the limbo or liminal space represented by the camps in Jordan or Turkey. Now they were in Australia seeking to build a new life (ideal future), but their present was somewhat fraught or equivocal as they struggled with loneliness, language and the shock of new culture. Simultaneously there was a longing for the lives and friendships they once had (living in the past).

As these letters literally travelled across borders, territories and places, they also travelled across time. It was as if the storylines of past, present and future had a chance to produce harmony rather than discord: that if these young people in the present could contribute ('energy for a month') to people in situations similar to those they were in only recently, then this could provide a sense of continuity rather than dislocation.

This particular sort of travel/traffic made something else possible. Building on the sense of accomplishment and pride I sensed in the students after they had heard the letter from Kilis, I asked if they would be willing to create a new letter, this time for Syrian students who will arrive at Adelaide Secondary School of English in the future. By now, these students had been at the school for a couple of months, perhaps they would be happy to share some of what they have learnt about making a new life in Adelaide?

Paul Coats, the school counsellor, suggested we take turns so that each student could offer one tip to new students, or one place they would welcome them to. This is the document we created:

What we've learnt about making a new life in Adelaide: Tips for those who will be arriving soon

We are a group of young Syrians who arrived in Adelaide four to six months ago. Some of us have already made many new friends here. Some of us are still looking for friends. And some of us are really missing our friends back home.

We have put together some of our ideas to share with other young people who might be arriving here soon. Here are our tips and our ideas about how we wish to welcome you. We hope these ideas are helpful.

- When you first arrive, I would like to take you on a tour of this school and particularly show you the classrooms.

- I'd like to show you the library – it's an important place for me here.

- I will introduce you to all the other Syrian students here. We will look out for you. And you can start looking out for people who one day might become your friends.

- I'd like to tell you that Australia is beautiful. It is like our country.

- When you arrive, I will take you to taste the ice-cream at McDonald's. It's very creamy and nice.

- When you first arrive you will probably miss your friends. I miss my friends in Jordan very much.

- At first you may have difficulties with language, but remember, we are safe here and the people are friendly. This gives us hope that there is life to live.

- When you first come to school you will see that some people have a lot of information that they are trying to teach you. There is so much to learn! It can be overwhelming. But if you just take it step by step it gets easier.

- At first you might feel lost, but we can feel safe from war here. It's a place where you can achieve your dreams.

- When I first arrived it was like a dream. This dream had been in my head for so long and I couldn't believe I had made it. Then, slowly, slowly, I started to miss my country. And I started to miss talking in Arabic. When you arrive you will probably feel many different things at different times.

- The first thing I will show you when you arrive is how to get your driver's licence! It is a very different process here. It's exciting to get your licence!

- I will show you how to take the bus. Even if you have no English, you can take the bus. I will help with translation.

- If you are thinking of coming to Australia, I recommend you learn English before you get here. If you don't speak English here it is very hard, so start learning now.

- I think it's good to remember that wherever you go, wherever you are, the most beautiful place will always be your country.

We've been here in Adelaide now for four to six months. These are some of the ways in which we want to welcome you. We are awaiting your arrival.

With warmth,
From your Syrian (soon-to-be) friends at
Adelaide Secondary School of English.

About this letter: writing a place to live

Again, this is a double-storied letter. It honours not only the blossoming knowledge of these young people in relation to making a life in a new country, but also continuing heartbreak and sorrow in relation to the loss of friends and speaking in one's mother tongue. There were tears on one student's face as she spoke of missing her friends.

This process made a sort of writing possible for young people who were struggling with and between languages and who, in a new country, often had very limited ways to have a say on matters of their own identity. Theodor Adorno once wrote that for a person 'who no longer has a homeland, writing becomes a place to live' (Adorno, 2002, p. 61). There were moments in the process of creating this letter together that the young students seemed to be actively writing a place to live. This seemed particularly true in the ways they found language to honour Syria and Australia simultaneously:

I'd like to tell you that Australia is beautiful. It is like our country.

And then later through this echoed lament:

I think it's good to remember, that wherever you go, wherever you are, the most beautiful place will always be your country.

In these concepts that were 'found' in the process of writing to those yet to arrive, these young Syrians were creating a place in which to live.

I read back the draft of this letter just before the bell rang to signal the end of the lesson. While some students started to move towards the exit, one moved to the table up the front where I was sitting. When Paul, the school counsellor, asked if she wanted to add something further to the letter, she said, 'No, I want to take a photograph of the letter from Turkey and our letter to them'. She took out her mobile phone and did so. We also agreed to translate all the letters into Arabic so they could be shared with the students' families and beyond.

Families and intergenerational honouring

There is one further part of this process that I wish to convey. When families move countries, relations between the generations face many challenges. Parents, children and young people face different restraints in learning a new language. They adapt differently to new cultural ways and, in Australia, some may experience different expressions of racism and Islamophobia. All these factors can increase the chances of intergenerational conflict, and it therefore becomes vital to foster what I call contexts for intergenerational honouring (Denborough, 2010a).

This awareness informed each letter that was created in this project. In the first conversation with the two brothers, I specifically asked, 'What about different ways you support each other within your family? Does an older brother have particular responsibilities? Are there particular ways that children support parents and parents support children?'

In our family, we had to keep encouraging each other. Older brothers take the harder work and most of the responsibility. My father is a completely new English learner. He is studying now and sometimes he is struggling with his homework so I try to explain things for him. He speaks Arabic and French and he is teaching my younger brother French. Finding other Arabic speakers was very good for my mother. And spending time together was important. In our first house we didn't have internet connection, we had to use mobile data, and this actually made us spend more time with each other. It turned out to be a good thing. After a while, my mum, my dad and my brother, we all started to volunteer to help new arrivals. To meet people at the airport. It was good doing this together.

The newly arrived students echoed a sentiment of 'encouraging each other' and 'learning together':

We also agree that we need to encourage each other in our families. We help our parents especially in how to speak English. We are learning together. This is our life. We have faced many hardships, and still are, but we have to encourage each other.

Shortly after I had shared the letter from Kilis with the students, I received a request from Shaista Kalaniya from the Muslim Women's Association. Shaista mentioned that a number of Syrian mothers who had recently moved to Adelaide had been experiencing Islamophobic harassment. She wondered if we could visit and speak with them. When Cheryl White and I visited, we mentioned that we had a letter that Syrian students at Adelaide Secondary School of English had written about their tips for making a new life in Australia and asked whether they would like to hear it. Many women's eyes lit up as they said that their children were at this school, and one mother, with pride and excitement stated, 'My daughter wrote that letter. She told me about it. Here is a photo of her. You must know my daughter'. And so I did, she was the young woman who had photographed all the letters.

As the letter was read, at one point the translator had to pause. She was so moved by the young people's words. She regained her composure and we continued. The mothers all said they wanted to send a response to the students.

Hello.

We are a group of Syrian mothers meeting at the Muslim Women's Association here in Adelaide. Today we heard the letter that you wrote at Adelaide Secondary School of English.

Some of you are our children!

There were 15 of us mothers listening today and also five small children. We think your letter says it all.

Some parts were very moving to us. Even though you are young, it is like you are speaking for us. Home will always be home. We also miss our friends.

The person who was translating for us today was very moved when you said that you miss speaking Arabic. Some of us had some tears as we listened to your words.

Sometimes here, I have felt as if I am the only sane person in a big insane group. When I said this, many other mothers laughed and agreed with me. So I realised maybe there are some other sane people too!

We also laughed when we heard how much you like the McDonald's creamy ice-cream.

And we smiled when we heard about you getting your driver's licence. We are about to learn how to get our L-plates.

One of us spoke about how she hopes one day to return to Syria, after the war is over, and she hopes you can visit her there.

One of us spoke about how, as a mother, she wants to heal and cure herself so that she can heal and cure her children. It can be very hard to make a new life.

> Some of us spoke of how we have only been in Australia for five months but now we are starting to feel more confident. Just as you are.
>
> You have only been here for four to six months but now you are thinking about how to welcome others.
>
> We are proud of you.
>
> Your letter says it all.

This exchange of letters that 'say it all' is one small initiative to support the efforts of young Syrians and their families in making lives in a new land. It is shared here in the hope it may provide possibilities for other contexts, and to provide a wider audience for the sparkling ideas and know-how of young Syrians.

It won't be too long before some of these young students are welcoming new arrivals, showing them the library, tasting ice-creams and sharing sorrow about lost or missing friends.

Arab children
Spring rain . . .
You are the generation
That will overcome defeat
– Nizar Qabbani

Acknowledgments

I would like to acknowledge the dedication and skills of teachers at the Adelaide Secondary School of English in general, and in particular, Anti Macri, Bronywn McClelland and Paul Coats. I'd also like to acknowledge the leadership of Shaista Kalaniya at the Muslim Women's Association of South Australia.

Notes

1. 'Communitas' is a particular form of connectedness that preserves individual distinctiveness (Turner, 1969, 1979). I describe its relevance to collective narrative practice in Denborough (2008).

2. The Dulwich Centre Foundation team that travelled to Turkey consisted of Cheryl White, David Newman and David Denborough. We were hosted by Mehmet Dinc who runs a yearlong narrative therapy training program in Turkey.

3. See   www.aljazeera.com/indepth/opinion/2016/05/turkey-kilis-rare-refugee-integration-160511102644814.html

PART II

DIVERSIFYING AND DEMOCRATISING NARRATIVE PRACTICE: FOLK CULTURAL METHODOLOGIES

It is now just over 10 years since the first folk cultural narrative methodology was developed: the Tree of Life narrative approach (Denborough, 2008; Ncube, 2006). Since then, the idea of combining narrative practice with a metaphor from treasured local cultural life has been embraced by practitioners and communities. Colleagues in many different contexts have now developed exquisitely diverse forms of metaphoric narrative practice. These include:

- Team of Life
  (see www.dulwichcentre.com.au/team-of-life; Denborough, 2008)

- Seasons of Life (Abu-Rayyan, 2009)

- Recipes of Life (Rudland-Wood, 2012)

- Crossing the River (Hegarty, Smith, & Hammersley, 2010)

- Kite of Life (Denborough, 2010a)

- Rhythm of Life
  (see www.dulwichcentre.com.au/rhythm-of-life-by-adriana-muller)

- Narratives in the Suitcase (Ncube-Mlilo, 2014)

- Smartphone of Life (Tse, 2016)

- Bicycle of Life (Leger, 2016)

- Beads of Life (Portnoy, Girling, & Fredman, 2015)

- Mat of Life and Fair Winds, informed by wrestling and sailing metaphors developed in Brazil by Lúcia Helena Abdulla and Recycling Minds.

The popularity of these approaches has been very surprising, at times even baffling, to me. Upon reflection, perhaps there are a number of different reasons for their resonance:

Speaking through metaphor: not having to speak in the first person

These approaches were initially developed to enable children and young people to address significant hardship or trauma they had experienced in ways that were not retraumatising. Significantly, metaphoric narrative practice doesn't require people to speak in the first person about the hardships. It enables meaning to be conveyed through metaphor rather than direct speech. As a young person, there is no way I would have spoken directly about tough or complex times I went through. Speaking through metaphor, however, may have offered different possibilities.

Starting with a treasured theme

These methods are infused with key narrative principles in relation to responding to trauma (Denborough, 2006; M. White, 2006c). This includes creating a 'safe territory of identity' (M. White, 2006b) or 'riverbank position' from the outset. This is achieved by speaking about treasured aspects of ordinary life: sports, kites, cooking, the natural world and so on. It is an easy and enlivening place to start – for both practitioners and those who meet with us. I'll always recall the feedback from young people of refugee backgrounds about these ways of working. They asked me to pass on to future facilitators to 'remember it's all about having fun'. This was particularly significant coming from these young folks who had endured significant sorrows, and whose Teams of Life had honoured various family members who had died in wars. They demonstrated to me that double-story development (including the acknowledgment and sharing of significant sorrow) actually becomes much more possible when we are also joined with each other in fun.

Diversifying narrative practice: cross-cultural inventions

The development of these methodologies was spurred by the following questions or challenges:

- How can narrative therapy be used in contexts where therapy is either not possible (due to lack of resources) or not culturally resonant?

- Can cross-cultural inventions and partnerships enable narrative practices to be used in ways that limit the likelihood of psychological colonisation?

The imposition of outsider healing knowledges has been powerfully critiqued by many writers (Arulampalam, Perera, de Mel, C. White, & Denborough, 2006; NiaNia, Bush, & Epston, 2017; Pupavac, 2001, 2002a, 2002b, 2006; Tamasese, 2002a, 2002b; Waldegrave, 1998; Watters, 2010). Forming cross-cultural partnerships and then developing methodologies that are based on resonant *local* metaphors can strengthen and richly story *local* healing knowledges. Perhaps basing our work on local folk cultural metaphors can make it more possible to engage in rich story development in culturally resonant ways. Hopefully, taking local folk culture as a starting point for our practice can contribute to diversifying narrative practice.

Democratising narrative practice

These folk cultural methodologies were also deliberately developed so that narrative therapy and community work ideas can be engaged with, not only by highly trained professionals, but also by key community and family leaders who may not have had the privilege of extensive schooling or education. This is what I refer to as democratising narrative practice. How can we ensure that narrative ways of working can be put into practice by aunties, uncles, mothers, fathers and community leaders, especially in contexts where highly trained professionals may be few and far between? This ethic of accessibility has enabled practitioners to partner with concerned community members who may not be trained in counselling or community work. Indeed, some of the most sparkling projects currently taking place are led by community members and peer workers.

Creating imagery and words at the same time

I have come to realise that accompanying the spoken word with the co-creation of visual image and written text brings possibilities for identity development of which I was once unaware. These realms of visual narrativity have become vitally interesting to me and are explored in Chapter 5.

Extending a narrative therapy tradition: folk psychology to folk culture

Whereas the culture of the professional psychological disciplines generally requires us to turn away from "'ordinary", everyday and historical associations' (White, 1997, pp. 12–13), David Epston and Michael White were inspired by the work of Jerome Bruner (1990) to locate their narrative explorations within traditions of 'folk psychology' – the local meanings, preferences and ways of understanding life that people bring to the counselling room (see M. White, 2001a). I believe these metaphoric methods follow this lead and make it possible to build links between the realms of 'healing' and the realms of folk culture. Any valued aspect of local folk culture (from cooking to the natural world to kite flying) holds significant meaning for those who treasure it. It has become clear that these meanings can be unpacked and used to scaffold transformative conversations about life and identity. In this way, many of us have become interested in turning to everyday folk culture as a site of practice (see Denborough, 2008).

As practitioners continue to invent further folk cultural narrative methodologies, it seems relevant to examine the particular local circumstances in which they were first created. Chapter 3 traces the histories of the Tree of Life narrative approach, and makes visible some of the thinking that informed its development. I hope that this will further a determination to continually unearth and create ways of working that are resonant and relevant to particular contexts, thus contributing to an ever-diversifying field of narrative practice, rather than simply replicating any of these methodologies across contexts.

Chapter 4 provides an example of how the Team of Life narrative approach has been used to enable young people to speak about racism.

Chapter 5 is a more theoretical exploration of how these methodologies involve the creation of visual images as a way of constructing and conveying a preferred identity and therefore involve a particular 'visual narrativity' – a joining of image and story in deliberate ways.

Chapter 3

Tracing the roots of the
Tree of Life narrative approach

It was Ncazelo Ncube-Mlilo's idea to combine narrative practices with the metaphor of the Tree of Life (Timmel & Hope, 1984). Neither of us could have imagined where this idea would lead! Over the last 10 years, the Tree of Life narrative approach (Denborough, 2008; Ncube, 2006) has come to be used by counsellors and community workers in many different contexts with people of all ages (see www.dulwichcentre.com. au/the-tree-of-life/).

Significantly, practitioners from diverse cultures and religions are continually transforming this way of working by embedding it in local cultural traditions and community practices. This is beautifully illustrated by the recent adaptions by Muslim practitioners Ola Elhassan and Lobna Yassine (2017).

Also noteworthy is how many Tree of Life initiatives are peer-led or co-led through partnerships between professionals and community members. In Sweden, for example, Torbjörn Vennström trained parents whose children are in foster care to facilitate the Tree of Life with their own children and arranged for the foster carers to act as outsider witnesses to this process.[1] This is a sparkling example of how the Tree of Life narrative approach is being used as a way of empowering community members as facilitators. This is also true in peer mental health work in the UK (see pp. 67–69) and in Australia (Swan, 2016).

A number of practitioners have used the Tree of Life as a departure point to create their own distinct methodologies. The idea of combining local folk cultural metaphors with narrative practice has now sparked the development of a wide range of metaphoric innovations.[2] A recent example is Vanessa Davis's Aboriginal Australian methodology, 'My Meeting Place' (2017). These are all developments that we could not have predicted.

With so many different initiatives currently under way, it seems an appropriate time to trace the histories or 'roots' of the Tree of Life narrative approach. There are four reasons why I have chosen do this:

- I hope that by unpacking the thinking that informs how metaphor and narrative practice are intertwined in the Tree of Life this will assist those who are currently developing their own metaphoric methodologies.

- Transparently documenting the histories of any concept or method is a factor in seeking to avoid psychological colonisation or the imposition of any methodology from one context to another without adaption and/or transformation.

- I hope this telling of history will acknowledge some lesser known contributions. This chapter began as a letter I wrote to Sally Timmel after the death of Anne Hope[3] to acknowledge Sally and Anne's vital contributions to the development of initial Tree of Life exercise.

- Having seen the Tree of Life narrative approach become embraced by so many people, I have become intrigued about why this has happened. This piece seeks to acknowledge some of the diverse and profound cultural resonances that I think partly explain why this particular metaphor is so meaningful to so many.

Histories

Just over 10 years ago, the Regional Psychosocial Support Initiative (REPSSI),[4] an influential organisation that works throughout southern and eastern Africa to support communities to respond to vulnerable children, invited a number of us to visit Masiye children's camp in Zimbabwe.[5] This invitation was particularly instigated by Ncazelo Ncube-Mlilo, a Zimbabwean psychologist who was studying narrative approaches to therapy and community work at Dulwich Centre here in Australia. Ncazelo was hoping to find ways of engaging with narrative practices to enhance REPSSI's work with vulnerable children (see Ncube, 2006).

During our stay at Masiye Camp, Ncazelo Ncube-Mlilo, Noreen Huni, Siphelile Kaseke, Carmel Gaillard and others from REPSSI introduced us to the worlds of the children who were attending the camp, many of whom had lost multiple loved ones due to HIV/AIDS and were now living in profoundly challenging circumstances. We witnessed the dedication of the camp counsellors, all formerly 'vulnerable children' themselves, and saw how the children treasured their time at Masiye.

We also witnessed how the camp counsellors were using a Tree of Life metaphor to assist children to speak about their lives. Ncazelo had been introduced to this metaphor by a friend and colleague, Jonathan Brakarsh, when they were collaborating to find ways of facilitating community conversations about the psychosocial needs of children. At the time, I did not know where this idea had originated.[6] But later, I learnt that this was linked to the highly influential popular education handbook by Sally Timmel and Anne Hope, *Training for transformation* (Timmel & Hope, 1984).

While the children clearly enjoyed drawing their trees, we also came to vividly appreciate a number of concerns that Ncazelo Ncube-Mlilo had about some of the inadvertent effects of the process (see Ncube, 2006). Two aspects of Tree of Life process (as it was being used at Masiye Camp at that time) seemed particularly fraught. The 'leaves of the tree' were being used to represent friends and family members, but anyone who had passed away was being represented as a 'falling' or 'fallen' leaf. When it came time for children to then speak to others about their tree, we saw quite heartbroken children with relatively bare trees surrounded by many fallen leaves. These retellings seemed to be leaving children bereft. We also saw that the image or concept of 'bugs' was being used to represent difficulties or problems faced by the tree. As these were written directly onto the tree there seemed little distance between children's identities and any problems they were facing.

Other aspects of the tree making and sharing process seemed to be working well. Most significantly, the children clearly felt significant connections with trees, connections that I assume were not only personal, but perhaps also, to differing degrees, collective, cultural and spiritual.

We had been invited to work together with Ncazelo, REPSSI, the camp counsellors and the children at the camp to try to fashion a way in which the children could, in the words of Aboriginal Elder and narrative practitioner Aunty Barbara Wingard, 'tell their stories in ways that make them stronger' (Wingard & Lester, 2001).

Having watched what was already working, and what was inadvertently 'retraumatising',[7] I proposed a number of additions or changes to what had been taking place:

- altering what particular parts of the Tree of Life represent

- finding ways to use narrative practices to richly story preferred identities throughout the Tree of Life process

- creating a four-part process: Tree of Life, Forest of Life, Storms of Life, Ritual of Celebration.

I'll just briefly explain the thinking that informed each of these changes and additions, and how the process now works.

Altering what particular parts of the Tree of Life represent

The two most significant changes related to the 'bugs' and the 'leaves'. First of all, I suggested removing the 'bugs' or problems from the metaphor entirely (problems and difficulties are now spoken of collectively in the Storms of Life section). Second, we now ensure that within the 'leaves' section people who are no longer living are represented in the same way as those who are living. This means that connections with and contributions of the no longer living are richly honoured.[8]

Significantly, if at any time during this process children talk about treasured people who have passed away and are upset about this, we provided the camp counsellors with the following three questions to ask:

- Did you have lovely times with this person? Can you tell me about these?

- What was special about this person to you? What did they give to you?

- Would this person like it that you remember them and that you put them on your tree?

Figure 2. A Forest of Life from Ltyentye Apurte School in the Northern Territory, Australia ('Ltyentye Apurte' means a small grove of trees)

Grief is never only about loss; it is also about honouring. These questions, and a Tree of Life process that includes the no longer living as leaves remaining on the tree, gave the children a chance to honour those who have passed away, and to consider the ongoing contribution that they can make to a loved one by remembering them and by placing them as a leaf on their Tree of Life. This has significantly altered the sense of heartbreak that was associated with the 'fallen leaves' metaphor.

Finding ways to use narrative practices to richly story a sense of preferred identity throughout the Tree of Life process

The ways in which the tree metaphor is now structured enable us to make rich back-and-forth linkages between the roots (heritage), trunk (what is valued, skills) and branches (hopes and dreams). We encourage practitioners to ask questions about the histories of values and skills, and about the histories of dreams. This, in turn, can unearth previously unspoken or unrecognised heritage, which is then written on the trees' 'roots'. What is named as a present skill, value or dream may now become linked with legacies carried forth from grandparents, ancestry or community. This interweaving between present, past and future contributes to what we refer to as a 'reauthoring' of identity (M. White, 2007).

Creating a four-part process: Tree of Life, Forest of Life, Storms of Life and Ritual of celebration and acknowledgment

The most significant change to what was previously occurring at Masiye Camp was to place the creation of individual Trees of Life into a wider four-part process. After children make their individual trees these are now gathered together into a 'Forest of Life' before any individual retelling takes place. This generation of the Forest of Life involves the 'invention of unity in diversity' (Freire, 1994 p. 157).[9]

Within the Storms of Life section, we seek to provide a context for conscientisation (Freire, 2000). This is facilitated by externalising the difficulties or hazards faced by children and by using metaphor to do so. First, we consult the children about their knowledge of the difficulties and dangers that trees and forests face in their contexts and in different parts of the world. Through metaphor, we learn of many difficulties. Ncazelo Ncube-Mlilo reported that children in Soweto listed the 'burning of trees, cutting trees down, wee weeing on trees, kicking trees, too much rain, lightning, aging: trees can get old and die, and having no water' (Ncube, 2006, p. 13).

Having spoken of the difficulties faced by trees, we then consult the children about their knowledge of the dangers and difficulties that children face in their context and in different parts of the world. This is not seeking individual disclosure, but rather collective disclosure:

> These included: rape, being abused, abandonment, swearing at children, neglect, denying food, chasing children away from home, kidnapping, killing children, children living on the streets, children smoking glue, children having to sell their bodies for sex, and children not listening to their parents and caregivers. (Ncube, 2006, p. 13)

Importantly, we also enquire of children whether trees are to blame for the difficulties and hazards they encounter. After children have stood in solidarity with trees – 'NO, trees are not to blame!' – we then invite the children to stand in solidarity with each other in stating that 'NO, children are not to blame' when these Storms of Life make an appearance.

Within the field of narrative practice, Michael White (2006b) drew attention to the ways in which children are never passive recipients of hardship or trauma (this is also true for adults and communities). Finding ways to make their responses to hardship more visible and acknowledged can contribute to possibilities for further action. In order to make it more possible for children's *responses* to the Storms of Life to be identified and spoken about, we initiate a discussion about how animals respond to storms. A long list of ways in which animals respond to storms can be generated. This might include skills in hiding, protecting each other, flying away, running away, burrowing deep in the ground, building a nest, huddling together and so on. Children are often very knowledgeable about these sorts of things! By acknowledging and speaking about how animals are not simply passive when storms hit forests, this makes it possible for children to consider the ways in which they are not simply passive in the face of difficulties in their lives. Once the facilitator has a sense that the children are ready, the group can then be asked, 'Okay, well these are some of the ways in which animals respond to storms, what about how children respond to storms that come into their lives? What do children do when these hazards and storms come into their lives? Are there ways that they respond? Are there things that they do? Do they try to protect themselves and others like the animals do?' We can also ask what children, young people, adults and communities can do together to address and prevent these storms, and thereby use this process as a spark for broader social actions.

This is particularly relevant because the final part of the process involves a broader ritual to which key adults and community members are invited.

Children's ideas about ways of responding to 'Storms' have been featured in Reclaim the Night feminist antiviolence marches here in Australia. I'm really interested in how these processes can spark broader community conscientisation.

Figure 3. The first graduates of the Tree of Life narrative approach (Soweto)
Source: Ncazelo Ncube-Mlilo

Once we had developed the four-part Tree of Life process during our visit to Masiye Camp, Ncazelo Ncube-Mlilo facilitated this process in Soweto (see Ncube, 2006). REPSSI then created a freely available manual[10] and began to offer training workshops throughout southern and eastern Africa. And the approach also began to be taken up by narrative practitioners in different parts of the world.[11] So much so, there are now over 2500 members of the Tree of Life Facebook group![12]

Linking back to Sally Timmel, Anne Hope and the field of popular education

A couple of years after our time at Masiye Camp, I managed to track down a copy of the highly influential handbook, *Training for transformation: A handbook for community workers, Book 2* (Timmel & Hope, 1984). It features a Tree of Life trust-building exercise, which I assume was the spark that led the camp counsellors at Masiye to use this metaphor. All the developments I have mentioned here are therefore linked to this work! Here is the original version (see p. 65).

To my knowledge, this is the first published version of the use of the Tree of Life as a group work process and it evolved from the field of popular education. I'm hoping we might forge more connections between narrative practice and popular education.

Honouring cultural, spiritual and secular histories

Of course, the Tree of Life is an ancient concept, embedded within so many cultures, spiritualities and religions. The Tree of Life is mentioned in the books of Genesis and Revelation as a life-giving tree planted by God in the Garden of Eden to enhance and perpetually sustain the physical life of humanity.[13] The earliest image and text version that I can find is of a Hebrew Kabbalistic tree of life[14] by the Jesuit scholar Athanasius Kircher, produced between 1652 and 55 (Lima, 2014, p. 18). No doubt Indigenous

TRUST BUILDING

4. TREE OF LIFE

A tree, like a river, is one of the universal symbols of life. This exercise helps people reflect on their own lives in greater depth.

Procedure

a. Ask each person to close their eyes and imagine what kind of tree represents their life as they experience it now. It might be a very strong oak, a weeping willow, a faithful mango tree or a young sapling.

b. Ask each person to draw the tree of their own life.

  i. The roots represent
- The family from which we come,
- Strong influences which have shaped us into the person we are now

  ii. The trunk represents the structure of our life today
- Job
- Family
- Organisations, communities, movements to which we belong.

  iii. The leaves represent our sources of information
- Newspapers
- Radio, television
- Books
- Reports
- Friends and contacts

  iv. The fruits represent our achievements
- Projects we have organised
- Programs
- Groups we have started or helped to develop
- Materials we have produced

  v. The buds represent our hopes for the future. Thorns can represent the difficulties in our life

c. Give the group about 20 minutes to do this.

d. Share in groups of 3–5. If possible, it is good to do this in an open-ended session (e.g. in the evening) when groups can continue to share for as long as they wish.

Time   At least one hour
Materials   Paper and crayons for all participants

Figure 4. The Tree of Life exercise from Training for Transformation
       Source: Timmel & Hope, 1984, p. 38

cultures in Africa, Australia and beyond have been using tree metaphors for far longer. Aboriginal practitioners here in Australia are now engaging with and adapting the Tree of Life approach for their contexts as part of a broader project of decolonisation and developing culturally relevant and resonant practices for language reclamation (Johnson, 2015) and community healing and transformation (Dulwich Centre Foundation, 2008).

Secular and ecological uses of the Tree of Life metaphor have also been influential. Charles Darwin, for example, used the Tree of Life in 1859 to describe relationships between organisms (see Pietsch, 2013).

The significance of people's connections to trees continues to surprise and move me. When I was teaching in Kurdistan, I was alerted to the Arabic book, *The tree of being: An ode to the perfect man*, by the great Islamic scholar, Ibn 'Arabi (1165-1240). Kurdish colleagues made links between Ibn 'Arabi's writings and the ways in which they readily see life through tree metaphors:

Our life in Kurdistan is just like the life of a forest that has been destroyed many times by the previous Baath regime. They destroyed Kurdistan villages, forests and agricultural lands. They created fear; terror in the mothers and their children.

But after the process of the liberation of Kurdistan, there is now regrowth … new ground, new trunks, branches and leaves.

In Kurdistan, the tree is a symbol of life and of hope. Trees represent endurance, stability, power and continuation. They are deeply rooted into the earth and they reach into the sky.

In autumn, we see the leaves falling from the trees, but we know before too long there will be new leaves, new life. And when we see this new life, it brings relief and comfort.

Trees also provide for Kurdish families. They give us fruits and are a source of income for those who trade in the mountains.

There are spiritual meanings too. In the Holy Koran, there are olive trees and fig trees. In religion, the tree is sometimes a symbol of a good, reputable family.

And traditionally, trees are placed on people's graves.

What's more, we resemble trees. A tree begins as a child, and day by day it grows. Like the hopes we build in our hearts, a small tree needs protection until it grows.

And trees in Kurdistan must be strong to survive the elements. Trees teach us how to resist.

In fact, the symbol of the Kirkuk Centre for Torture Victims is a tree.

~ The counsellors of Kirkuk Center for Torture Victims[15] (Kirkuk Center for Torture Victims & Dulwich Centre Foundation International, 2012, p. 11)

In reflecting on these histories, and in talking with Ncazelo Ncube-Mlilo, we're now thinking about creating a tree image and text to represent the diverse histories of the Tree of Life narrative approach. The children of Masiye Camp and Soweto would be written on the roots, as would the camp counsellors of Masiye Camp, REPSSI, Ncazelo Ncube-Mlilo, David Denborough, Noreen Huni, Siphelile Kaseke, Carmel Gaillard, Anne Hope and Sally Timmel, Paulo Freire, Michael White, David Epston, Cheryl White, Jonathan Brakarsh, Barbara Wingard, Shona Russell, the Just Therapy Team and Dulwich Centre.

The branches of the Tree of Life represent hopes, dreams or wishes. I hope this short history can spark yet further adaptions and the creation of new forms of metaphoric narrative practice. I hope it might encourage you to notice some aspect of treasured local folk culture in your own context, craft this into metaphor, infuse it with narrative practice principles, and in so doing create your own form of practice.

Dreaming of mobile counselling teams in South Africa

In recent years, Ncazelo Ncube-Mlilo has continued to develop creative narrative practice methodologies. These have included combining the Suitcase Project (Clacherty, 2006; Clacherty, Suitcase Storytellers, & Welvering, 2006) with narrative practice and journey metaphors (see www.dulwichcentre.com.au/suitcase). More recently, working in partnership with six women living in informal settlements in northern Johannesburg, Ncazelo has developed the COURRAGE methodology. COURRAGE is a collective narrative way of working that has been developed to privilege the alternative stories of women who have faced significant hardships. It seeks to honour the strengths, skills and courage women show and use in the face of sorrow and grief. This methodology draws significantly from the work of Linda Tuhiwai Smith (1999) in which she describes 25 indigenous projects. Through the organisation PHOLA, Ncazelo is working to create mobile therapeutic counselling and development services that can reach the most disadvantaged and marginalised communities. By the year 2020 she aims to bring hope and restore the lives of at least 10 000 women and girls using the COURRAGE methodology. To learn more about this and/or to support this initiative, please contact ncazelo@yahoo.com

How REPSSI has used the Tree of Life

In 2005, REPSSI and Dulwich Centre published a manual for the Tree of Life. This project was led by Ncazelo Ncube-Mlilo of REPSSI and David Denborough of Dulwich Centre. REPSSI works in 13 countries in eastern and southern Africa using the Tree of Life. REPSSI has trained a significant number of skilled facilitators among REPSSI's implementing partners. For example, in Swaziland, the Tree of Life has been used in kids' clubs to help vulnerable children to identify and discuss their social connectedness, and to explore their strengths, skills and talents. In the same country, the Tree of Life has been used in training caregivers who work in neighbourhood care points. The Tree of Life has enabled the caregivers to understand the individual children they work with, and to identify the social relationships (within peer groups, families, clans and communities) that can be harnessed to maximise the care and protection of these children. In Botswana, the Tree of Life has been used extensively for retrospection and introspection before introducing other approaches. It has been used during psychosocial support camps for group counselling with children. In Tanzania, it has been used extensively as a self-awareness tool for facilitators before introducing other modules. Also in Tanzania, the Tree of Life has been used to support abused children who are passing through the casualty department. Save the Children in Tanzania uses the the Tree of Life as a case management tool to strengthen child protection processes. Finally, in South Africa, Tree of Life has been used in an after school club in Soweto to strengthen bonds and understanding between grandmothers and the grandchildren they are raising. The challenge for the grandparents was communication with their grandchildren who were misbehaving. The other challenge was that most of the children did not understand why they were being raised by their grandparents. The Tree of Life helped the children and grandparents to appreciate each other and enhanced communication.

Diverse Tree of Life initiatives in the UK

Many different communities in the UK have embraced the Tree of Life narrative approach in sparkling ways. So much so that there have already been two conferences held in London to showcase local Forests of Life! What has perhaps been most significant is that many of these initiatives have involved partnerships between workers and community members and have been peer led or co-led. For those wanting to know more about this, I've included here a number of references and links.

Adults living with HIV

The first Tree of Life project in the UK was a community project initiated by Georgia Iliopoulou and co-led with adults living with HIV:

> Iliopoulou, G., Jovia, Kenny, Lucy, & Sandra. (2009). The tree of Life in a community context. *Context*, *105*, 50–54.

Building on this initiative, Georgia Iliopoulou, Heleni Andreadi and Glenda Fredman have offered training in the approach.

Peer and community mental health work

Angela Byrne was then inspired to initiate the Trailblazer project in collaboration with African and Caribbean men in the UK:

> Byrne, A., Warren, A., Joof, B., Johnson, D., Casimir, L., Hinds, C., Mittee, S., Jeremy, J., Afilaka, A., & Griffiths, S. (2011). "A powerful piece of work": African and Caribbean men talking about the "tree of life". *Context*, (October), 40–45.

Since then, service user co-produced Tree of Life groups have been formed within South London and Maudsley adult acute in-patient service: www.youtube.com/watch?v=ep9H4xL7lPo

Other peer mental health initiatives have been led by Yasmin Kapadia, Moeva Rinaldo and Cerdic Hall through Camden and Islington Recovery College.

Links with Uganda

The Tree of Life has been used to empower peer mental health champions in Uganda through Butabika–East London Link and Heartsounds Uganda:

Hall, C., Baillie, D., Basangwa, D., & Atakunda, J. (2016). Brain gain in Uganda: A case study of peer working as an adjunct to statutory mental health care in a low income country. In R. White, S. Jain, D. Orr, & U. Read (Eds.), *The Palgrave handbook for global mental health: Sociocultural perspectives*. London, England: Palgrave MacMillan.

To learn more about the broader Butabika–East London Link and Heartsounds Uganda see this video: www.thet.org/media/videos/butabika-east-london-link-mental-health-peer-support-champions

With older adults

Clayton, M., Fredman, G., Martin, E., Anderson, E., Battistella, S., Johnson, S., Milton, A., & Rapaport, P. (2012). Systemic practice with older people: Collaboration, community and social movement. *PSIGE Newsletter, 21*, 20–26.

With people with learning disabilities

Baum, S., & Shaw, H. (2015). The tree of life methodology used as a group intervention for people with learning disabilities. *The Bulletin, 13*(1), 14–19.

With children and young people

Casdagli, L., Christie, D., Girling, I., Ali, S., & Fredman, G. (in press). Evaluating the Tree of Life Project for Children and Young People living with Type 1 Diabetes at UCLH: An innovative way of engaging young people with Diabetes. *Diabetes Care for Children and Young People.*

German, M. (2013). Developing our cultural strengths: Using the 'Tree of Life' strength-based, narrative therapy intervention in schools, to enhance self-esteem, cultural understanding and to challenge racism. *Educational and Child Psychology, 30*(4), 75–99.

Hughes, G. (2014). Finding a voice through 'The Tree of Life': A strength-based approach to mental health for refugee children and families in schools. *Clinical Child Psychology and Psychiatry, 19*(1), 139–153.

With parents

McFarlane, F., & Howes, H. (2012). Narrative approaches to group parenting work: Using the tree of life with 'hard-to-reach' parents. *Context, 123,* 22–25.

Believe it or not, this is only a small glimpse of the diverse community Tree of Life initiatives in the UK! We are very much looking forward to seeing what continues to emerge in coming years.

Notes

1. See www.dulwichcentre.com.au/wp-content/uploads/2014/01/using-the-tree-of-life-in-family-work.pdf

2. These include: the Team of Life (see www.dulwichcentre.com.au/team-of-life; Denborough, 2008), Seasons of Life (Abu-Rayyan, 2009), Recipes of Life (Rudland-Wood, 2012), Crossing the River (Hegarty, Smith, & Hammersley,

2010), Kite of Life (Denborough, 2010a), Narratives in the Suitcase (Ncube-Mlilo, 2014), Smartphone of Life (Tse, 2016), Bicycle of Life (Leger, 2016), Beads of Life (Portnoy, Girling, & Fredman, 2015) and Mat of Life and Fair Winds informed by wrestling and sailing metaphors developed in Brazil by Lúcia Helena Abdulla and Recycling Minds.

3. To read more about the life of Anne Hope see www.iol.co.za/capetimes/anne-hope-a-woman-of-substance-in-anti-apartheid-movement-1964986

4. See www.repssi.org/about-us/

5. The Dulwich Centre team consisted of Michael White, Cheryl White, Shona Russell and me.

6. In her influential paper, 'The Tree of Life Project: Using narrative ideas in work with vulnerable children in southern Africa', Ncazelo Ncube-Mlilo describes how she had been introduced to the 'Tree of Life' by a colleague and friend, Jonathan Brakarsh (Ncube, 2006, p. 6).

7. I hesitate to use psychological terms developed in the West to describe experience elsewhere, but the scenes of the children retelling their trees, bereft of leaves, did seem to be quite a harrowing experience for both the children and witnesses.

8. This is linked to what are known as 'saying hullo again' (M. White, 1988a) or 're-membering' conversations (M. White, 2007) in narrative practice.

9. Sally Timmel and Anne Hope were profoundly influenced by Paulo Freire and the field of popular education has involved the practical implementation of Freirian principles. Our work at Dulwich Centre Foundation is also influenced by Paulo Freire. Although I am sure Freire would challenge us about whether we do enough to ensure that our ways of working are relevant to and resonant with the most marginalised, and also whether we are doing enough to speak and sustain social movement beyond the status quo (see Denborough, 2008; Freire, 1999).

10. Jonathan Morgan from REPSSI was influential in putting together this manual, which can be found here: www.pacificdisaster.net/pdnadmin/data/original/REPSSI_2007_Tree_life.pdf

11. See www.dulwichcentre.com.au/tree-of-life

12. See www.facebook.com/groups/TreeofLifeNarrativeApproach/

13. To read about the biblical Tree of Life, see Lanfer (2012).

14. According to Manuel Lima (2014, p. 18), a key element of Kabbalah wisdom is the Tree of Life, 'an image composed of a diagram of 10 circles, symbolising 10 pulses, or emanations, of divine energy'.

15. This centre has now changed its name to the Jiyan Foundation: www.jiyan-foundation.org

Chapter 4

Creating 'Justice Teams':
Unearthing young people's skills
in responding to racism

The Team of Life was the second metaphoric narrative folk methodology to be developed (Denborough, 2008). This chapter offers a glimpse of how these methodologies can be used collectively to respond to social issues such as racism.

It's a winter morning and we're in Dandenong, one of the most ethnically diverse suburbs in Australia. More than half the people who live around here were born overseas. They come from over 150 different countries and many are from non-English speaking backgrounds. Today we're visiting St John's Regional College, a high school that for the last six years has been using the Team of Life narrative approach to enable young men to speak through sporting metaphors about what and who is important to them. It was originally created to enable former child soldiers in Uganda to address experiences of profound hardship without having to talk directly about these experiences. Now it is being used in many different contexts.[1]

There's a group of us visiting Dandenong today. We're in the process of developing a Team of Life theatre production and the cast is heading to St John's Regional College to conduct a workshop with young men, many of whom have refugee backgrounds, and the majority of whom are Sudanese. The cast includes two Aboriginal performers: Kutcha Edwards (a singer/songwriter) and Heath Bergesen (an actor and didgeridoo player); three young Sudanese physical performers: Juima Deng, Nyuol Bol and Pier Akec; and Assmaah Helal, the reigning Muslim sportsperson of the year![2]

After an Aboriginal acknowledgment of country, a song by Kutcha Edwards and a dynamic physical warm-up, we introduce the Team of Life metaphor.

The Team of Life process

The Team of Life process involves inviting people to think about their life as if it were a sporting team, and to consider who makes up the membership of their Team of Life: 'These people can be alive or no longer living. They can be present in your life now or people who you have known in the past'.

more metaphors

Part 1: Who is in your Team of Life

Who are the people who have been most influential (in a positive way) in your life?

- Who is your goal keeper? If you had to name one person who looks out for you, who guards your goals, who is most reliable, who would this be?

- Who is your coach? Who have you learnt the most from? It is possible to have more than one coach. And it's possible that they may or may not still be alive. What are some of the things that they have taught you?

- Who are some of the other teammates in your life: those you play with, those whose company you enjoy?

- Who are your fans? Who is cheering you on? Who is hoping you and your team will do well?

As part of the process, 'teamsheets' are often drawn.

Figure 5. A Brazilian Team of Life teamsheet

Figure 6. A goal map drawn in Mt Elgon, Uganda

Inviting young people to consider their lives as a team generates a particular sense of identity. It is a sense of identity that features choice (as to whom they include), collectivity (as opposed to using internal, individualistic metaphors of the self), and continuity between the living and the no longer alive (which can be particularly significant for those from refugee backgrounds).

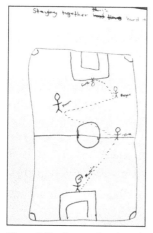

Figure 7. *'Staying together through hard times'*

Part 2: Goal maps and celebrations

The second step in the Team of Life process involves acknowledging and celebrating 'goals' that these teams have already scored. For instance, 'Staying together through hard times' (see left). We draw a 'goal map' acknowledging the achievement and then we celebrate it as if it were a goal in a sporting arena. This can involve commentating the goal, re-enacting it, and having people cheer on the team as if they were spectators or fans. This honouring of past goals involves generating and performing a collective heritage of achievement. Having done so, young people often then want to talk about, plan and train for future 'goals'. It is much easier to look forward once you have a collective heritage of achievement to build upon.

Part 3: Enabling contribution – sharing survival skills

A key principle of collective narrative practice involves enabling those who are enduring hardship to make contributions to the lives of others (Denborough, 2008). The third step in the Team of Life process therefore involves enabling young people to share their skills of survival and insider knowledge with others who are going through hard times. These exchanges take place between communities or even across countries.

On this particular morning in Dandenong, Assmaah Helal reads to the young people a collective document from the Aboriginal community of Yuendumu[3] about how the people of this community managed to bring peace after a number of years of great conflict. As she reads aloud, the young people listen with silent intensity. We then ask, 'What would you like to share back with the people of Yuendumu?'

As we tentatively begin to piece together a response to the people of Yuendumu, one young man asks, 'Have the people of Yuendumu had to deal with racism?' His question turns us in a different direction. After acknowledging the importance of his question, and answering that yes, the people of Yuendumu have had to deal with racism and its effects for over 150 years, it's vividly clear that this subject is resonating powerfully with the young people in the room.

And so, we decide to talk more about racism. More particularly, I begin to ask questions about how they, as young people in Dandenong, respond to racism, what sort of teamwork is required when you are up against racism, and what would they like to share with other young people who may also be facing racism in their lives. Over the next 15 minutes or so, different young people share their ideas with the cast. With their permission, I rescue their words on paper in order to create the following collective document. It consists of the hard-won knowledge of the young students at St John's, as well as contributions from Sudanese and Aboriginal cast members.

THE JUSTICE TEAM
'Don't let racism drag you down'
from St John's Regional College, Dandenong

Figure 8. The Justice Team from St John's Regional College

When you're up against racism, you need a team.
This is our team. This is what we do when racism is around.

Whatever they say about what country we are from, or whatever they say about what colour we are, we have skills in ignoring it. We don't listen to racism.

We remember to be proud of who we are, to be proud of our culture.

One of us said, 'For me, if someone gives me a hard time, if someone calls me a name, before I let it go into me, before I let it put me in a bad mood, I say "Hang on. He's being racist. No. You can have that back. I'm going to send that back. I'm sending that back with love". This really works for me. It's like sending back the negative energy. It's like a spiritual thing. There was this time I was working in a kitchen, and this man was being stupid, saying racist things. I said, "No, I'm not going to receive that. I'm going to send that back with love". And then the tomatoes he was chopping up suddenly started going all over the place! I was like, this really works!'

On our team, friends play a really important part. It's like they are the defence on our team and the midfield. Our friends encourage us; try to help us out. If racism is around, we talk to our friends. If we know someone has just copped it then we tell them positive things.

You see, if other people disrespect us then it's even more important that we show each other respect.

Our families are on this team too. They help us through hard times.

There are other important players too. Like Nelson Mandela. And don't forget God.

This is our team. And we've got a lot of stories.

One of us said, 'I play soccer. I'm a striker, pretty quick. I've worked it out now that the only time the defence gives me a hard time, the only time they start to abuse me with words, is when I am scoring goals. In the first game I played in, I got a red card.

I retaliated. But in the second game, when he tried to drag me down, I played my own game. And at the end, I shook his hand and he gave me a hug. Now, what I say to other people is when someone is trying to drag you down it means you are doing well. It means they are worried you are going to score goals. So don't let them drag you down ... just keep playing your game. That's what I tell myself too'.

After we heard this story we all clapped.

This is our team. We call it the Justice Team.

It helps us to hold onto pride and dignity. It helps us to remember good times, times we have spent with friends and family.

We come from many different places. And many of our families have had really hard times, in South Sudan, Mauritius and other places. So we know about keeping hopes up. We know about learning from mistakes. We know that after bad things good can sometimes come.

And we know that when you're up against racism, you need a team.

We hope you have a Justice Team too, wherever you are.

If not, maybe you can join our team. We're always looking for new members.

This collective document of young people's skills and knowledges in dealing with racism will now be shared with other young people in different parts of the country and overseas. We will facilitate an exchange of messages and knowledge among young people. We will also share this document with the people of Yuendumu, to let them know that it was their courage and determination to reclaim their community that inspired the articulation of this first 'Justice Team'.

A few weeks after our visit, the school counsellor at St John's Regional College, Milan Colic, met with the young people, and worked with them to depict their Justice Team visually, in a poster (see p. 84).

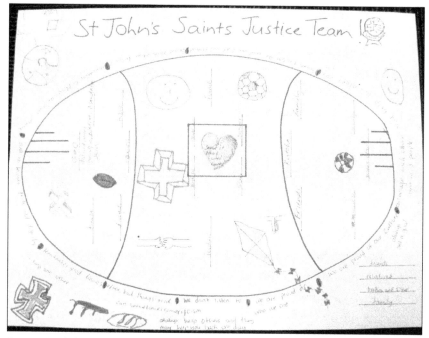

Figure 9. St John's Saints Justice Team poster

There was one other significant development from the day we visited Dandenong. A Team of Life group is now going to be set up for young women at St John's. Perhaps it's only a matter of time before a Gender Justice Team is also formed.[4]

The Team of Life approach has been developed for young people who have endured significant hardships, especially those who have witnessed events that are unspeakable. Through sporting metaphors and the use of narrative approaches, we have found that the Team of Life approach makes it possible for young people to 'tell their stories in ways that make them stronger' (Wingard & Lester, 2001).

Perhaps with the creation of Justice Teams, there's now the possibility of going one step further. By eliciting, documenting, honouring and circulating young people's skills and initiatives in responding to forms of injustice, perhaps this could in some modest way contribute to forms of 'social movement' (Denborough, 2008). As we are living in a society in which racism and gender injustice remain so prevalent, I do hope so.

Notes

1. For descriptions of how the Team of Life is being used in different contexts, see Denborough (2010c, 2012). See also: www.dulwichcentre.com.au/team-of-life. html and dulwichcentre.com.au/trying-not-to-fight-with-friends/

2. Other team members included Kate Denborough and Gerard van Dyck (co-creative directors of KAGE), Nyuol Bol, Rachel Elphick, Thomas Greenfield and Timothy Ohl. We visited St John's through the invitation of Milan Colic, one of the school psychologists who is also the facilitator of the Team of Life group in the school. To learn more about the Team of Life theatre production, see www.kage. com.au

3. Yuendumu is an Aboriginal community in the Northern Territory, Australia. If you would like to read a copy of the document from Yuendumu, write to daviddenborough@dulwichcentre.com.au

4. For more information about the use of narrative practices and considerations of gender justice, see Yuen & C. White (2007).

Chapter 5

Narrative practice and the image: Virtually engaging in the storylines of others

In trying to understand why narrative methodologies such as the Kite of Life, Tree of Life and Team of Life have been so warmly embraced by diverse communities, it's clear that there is something about the act of creating a visual representation of preferred identity that is significant. This chapter explores the interesting connections between narrative practice and visual imagery.

Histories of the image in narrative therapy

There is a long history of narrative therapists engaging in practices of 'visual narrativity' (Bal, 2008, p. 625) and then theorising about this. Michael White, for instance, drew on the work of Gaston Bachelard (1969) and William James (1890) to accentuate the significance of the image in his therapeutic encounters. Let me offer four brief examples of the use of images in narrative therapy:

- visualising the problem
- evoking the image
- focalising questions
- images of identity: revitalising a language of inner life.

Visualising the problem

In externalising conversations, developing a visual characterisation of the externalised problem is often influential in creating distance between it and the person's identity. This is perhaps most obvious in the ways narrative therapists invite children to draw pictures of the externalised problem (see M. White, 2007, Chapter 1).

Evoking the image

Within definitional ceremonies, outsider witnesses are asked to describe an image of the person at the centre of the ritual:

As you heard of the steps Fiona is taking to reclaim her life, what picture of her was evoked?

As you listened, what images of life came to mind?

Did you have any realisations about your own life?

How did this affect your picture of who you are as a person? (M. White, 2004b, pp. 51–52)

Focalising questions

Within narrative therapy consultations, 'hypothetical focalizing' (Herman, 2002) questions are asked to invite the person to look at their life from different angles or perspectives:

If you were seeing yourself through [your lost loved one's] eyes right now, what would you be noticing about yourself that you could appreciate?

What did your mother see when she looked at you through her loving eyes? (M. White, 1988a, p. 8)

Such visualisations are ways in which narrative momentum can be generated: 'Visuality … rivals action-generated events for dominance over the plot structure' (Bal, 2008, p. 629). There is a name within narrative theory for this plot-generation aspect of visuality. It's referred to as figuration: 'Figuration is a visualizing strategy of the narrative text' (Bal, 2008, p. 629).

Images of identity: revitalising a language of inner life

Discussing his work with people who had endured trauma, Michael White described his efforts to revitalise a person's 'language of inner life' (James, 1890) through renewing 'positive images of life and identity' (M. White, 2011, p. 128). This delicate and careful process involves revaluation and resonance. It is a process that Michael described in visual terms. By richly revaluing a person's responses to trauma, and what it is that they have held precious despite hardship, a particular sort of resonance is generated:

The resonance that is set off by these therapist-initiated responses to what a person accords value has the effect of evoking positive images of life and identity that often present to the person in metaphorical and visual forms. As these images build in these conversations, they have the potential to set off reverberations into the history of the person's experiences of life. At this time, the therapist can introduce an inquiry that identifies the way in which these reverberations touch on memories that are resonant with these images of the present ... It is in the linking of episodes of life through history that is provided by these resonances that new connections and patterns of experience are developed, and that unifying themes of life are identified and named through metaphor. This process sponsors the development of an inner world that can be visualized, and a sense of aliveness that displaces a sense of emptiness and deadness. (M. White, 2011, p.128)

Collective narrative practice and visual images

In recent years, a number of collective narrative practice methodologies, including the Tree of Life (Denborough, 2008; Ncube, 2006), the Kite of Life (Denborough, 2010a), the Team of Life (Denborough, 2008) and My Meeting Place (Davis, 2017), have combined the four visualising conversational narrative practices mentioned above with the creation of visual images in the form of paintings and drawings.

It has been surprising to me how this process and these visual narrative methodologies have been so embraced. It seems that representing one's preferred storyline through particular folk cultural symbols, and creating visual images depicting this, creates significant resonance in many different contexts. This process seems to warrant further examination: What is happening in this process? Why the resonance? How do these created visual images

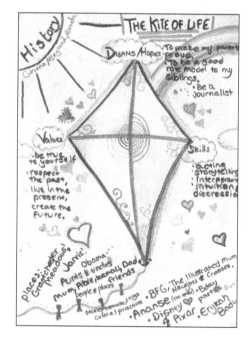

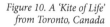

Figure 10. A 'Kite of Life'
from Toronto, Canada

relate to the creation of preferred storylines of identity? What is the role of visual imagery in this process? To consider this, let's examine some recent developments in narrative media studies.

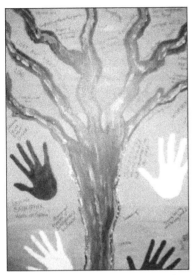

Figure 11. Tree of Life from the Tree of Life Women's Group in Elizabeth, South Australia Source: Jennifer Swan.

Figure 12. Tree of Life from the Tree of Life Women's Group in Elizabeth, South Australia Source: Jennifer Swan

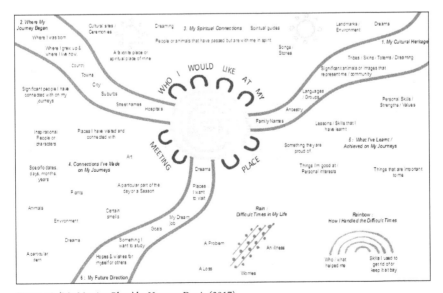

Figure 13. 'My Meeting Place' by Vanessa Davis (2017)

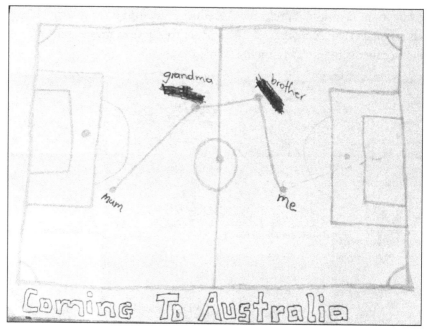

Figure 14. A goal map from young person who came to Australia as an 'unaccompanied minor'

Figure 15. Nihaya Abu-Rayyan with a team sheet from one of the women she works with in Hebron, Palestine

The new transmedial narrative theory

Although in some ways narratology, the formal study of narrative, was initially conceived as a project that could transcend disciplines and media, the study of narrative across media, or transmedial narrative studies, is relatively new. Transmedial narrative studies seeks to question 'how the intrinsic properties of the medium shape the form of narrative and affect the narrative experience' (Ryan, 2004, p. 1). This has become particularly relevant over the last few decades as theorists have been faced with the challenge of how to understand the new forms of narrative, storytelling and story-making that take place through interactive digital media:

The cultural salience of audio-visual media, the emergence of computer gaming and interactive media, digitization and networking – all of these have challenged narratologists to broaden their understanding of narrative so as to account for these new forms. As a result there has been a new interest amongst narrative theorists in the formative influence of particular media on the production of narratives (writing, film, photography, social networking sites). (Rigney, 2013, p. 197)

Transmedial theorists have begun to rigorously examine narrative within face-to-face narration, still pictures, moving pictures, music and digital media. In doing so, Marie-Lauren Ryan has made a helpful distinction between some media 'being a narrative' and others 'possessing narrativity':

The property of 'being' a narrative can be predicated on … the intent of evoking a narrative script in the mind of the audience. 'Having narrativity', on the other hand, means being able to evoke such a script. In addition to life itself, pictures, music, or dance can have narrativity without being narratives in a literal sense. (Ryan, 2004, p. 9)

The visual images created within the Tree of Life, Kite of Life, My Meeting Place or Team of Life processes do not in themselves convey a narrative script; however, they do possess 'narrativity' and the ways in which they facilitate new discussions and understandings demonstrate the vivid potential of this form of word-and-image storytelling. Before considering the synergies between narrative and imagery, however, it is worth noting the narrative limitations of the image.

Narrative limitations of the image

A number of theorists have pointed out the narrative limitations of images. These limitations are perhaps best summed up by the following quotes:

> In sum, a single picture can never actually represent a narrative but at best ... point to a story. (Wolf, 2005, p. 433)

One of the limitations is seen to be the inability of images to

> represent detailed alternative developments and characters' thought-worlds that eventually are not realized in the story. As a result, the suspense and the eventfulness which in verbal narratives often characterize such possibilities and the choices leading to their non-realisation get lost. (Wolf, 2005, p. 434)

I agree with both these statements, and would be surprised if any project that operated solely in the visual realm could generate rich description of preferred storylines of identity. However, as participants draw, share and discuss their trees, kites, meeting places and/or teams, alternative images of thought-worlds and identities are created. What makes this possible?

Images that reach into the past and future

The images that are created in collective narrative practice, whether these are Teams of Life, Kites of Life, Trees of Life or Meeting Places, are a 'unique blend of graphic and verbal signs' (Ryan, 2004, p. 143). One of the factors that enables them to contribute to alternative images of thought-worlds and identities is the way in which they reach into the past and future. By eliciting what is of value to people in the present, tracing the histories of these values, and then visually inscribing these histories in the iconic cultural representations of kites, trees or meeting places, images are created that reach into the past. By including people's hopes in these visual representations, this also evokes the future.

Why is this significant? One of the key features of narrative is double time structuring:

A salient property of narrative is double time structuring. That is, all narratives, in whatever medium, combine the time sequences of the plot events, the time of the histoire ('story-time') with the time of the presentation of those events in the text, which we call 'discourse-time.' What is fundamental to narrative, regardless of medium, is that these two time orders are independent. (Chatman, 1980, p. 122)

To increase the narrativity of team, kite, meeting place or tree images, it is therefore necessary to create a similar double sense of time. As participants share their 'narrative images' with others (in the present) they also invite one another into their histories and a double sense of time. This, I believe, transforms the narrative power of the imagery:

painting is strictly an art of the visible, which means that it is an art of the present, but … [when] painting can reach into the past and the future … [it transforms] itself from an art that speaks exclusively to the senses to an art that also speaks, like poetry, to the imagination. (Ryan, 2004, p. 25)

There is a second reason why this reaching into the past and future is significant. By tracing the histories of what people value, it becomes possible to create resonances between people's values (if not deeds). This is particularly significant when collective narrative practice projects seek to dissolve intergenerational conflicts and assist the development of intergenerational alliances (Denborough, 2010a). Whereas what members of the different generations actually do in their daily lives may vary enormously, eliciting what people give value to and tracing the histories of these values provides opportunities to bring the storylines of different generations into harmonic relationship.

Immersivity, interactivity and virtual involvement

There are three additional concepts from transmedial studies that also seem relevant to collective narrative practice projects. These are the concepts of 'immersivity', 'interactivity' and 'virtual involvement'. The first two of these are described by Ann Rigney (2013) as involving

> a shift of emphasis away from plot as a key feature of narrative to that of immersivity (digitization having provided new technologies for evoking virtual worlds) and interactivity (digitization having afforded new agency to users). (Rigney, 2013, p. 197)

And according to Fludernik (1996), becoming 'virtually involved' in the lives of others is a more essential feature of narrative than following an action to its completion:

> Thus 'narrative' is already no longer exclusively linked to the production of a coherent plot with a clearly defined beginning, middle and end, but also extends to include mediated ways of virtually engaging in other people's lives without these forming a 'plot' in a conventional sense. (Rigney, 2013, p. 198)

Within collective narrative practice projects, participants become immersed and virtually engaged in each other's lives, and interact with the storylines of others through many different mediums of storytelling and story-creating. Through processes of immersivity, interactivity and virtual involvement, we seek to enable a particular sense of unity: communitas. Communitas (Turner, 1969) is a shared sense of unity among individuals which:

- preserves individual distinctiveness

- is not a merging in fantasy

- does not depend on 'in-group versus out-group' opposition.

Developing a shared sense of unity across generations is invaluable in dissolving intergenerational conflict and enabling intergenerational alliances.

Sister arts – text and image

In this chapter, I have reflected on the history of narrative therapists' engagement in practices of 'visual narrativity' and introduced a number of concepts from transmedial studies. These are exciting times. Community projects in different parts of the world are resulting in new collective narrative practice methodologies. At the same time, interdisciplinary narratology is providing a 'growing domain of the parallel study of text and image' (Bal, 2008, p. 630).

The idea that narrative and imagery are essentially different cultural expressions [is now obsolete] … Narrative and image need each other as much as cultures need both of them. (Bal, 2008, p. 632)

As narrative practitioners, there seems a great deal to be gained through examining the 'culture of exchange between the two "sister arts"'– text and image (Bal, 2008 p. 630). I very much look forward to what we will discover!

PART III

CAN NARRATIVE PRACTICES SPARK AND SUSTAIN SOCIAL ACTION / SOCIAL MOVEMENT?

The following three chapters describe ways in which practitioners in diverse contexts are using narrative practices to respond to hardships and/or injustices to not only alleviate personal suffering, but also to spark social action/social movement to try to change local conditions.

Chapter 6 features the sparkling economic and environmental work of Caleb Wakhungu and the Mt Elgon Self-Help Community Project in rural Uganda. Chapter 7 considers how narrative practices can sustain activism and human rights work. Chapter 8 explores how collective testimonies and other narrative methodologies are being used to support social movements and community organising.

Chapter 6

Using narrative practice to spark diverse economic and environmental projects

This chapter describes how Caleb Wakhungu[1] in rural Uganda has been using collective narrative practices to spark and sustain diverse economic and environmental projects and at the same time contribute to the reinvigoration of local cultures. As Caleb describes, this way of working offers a significant challenge to conventional 'development' practice:

Development partners have always shown concern and sought to respond to reduce hardships that people in poverty are going through. However, their responses have been one sided. They have been looking at the affected population as 'poor' and 'vulnerable' and with nothing to offer as solutions to their own problems within environments they have lived in and mastered for generations!

The common development language has always been, 'these are poor people … they have nothing and so they need so much'. Interventions are then designed with little or no community participation and therefore recipients of such intervention have no choice of what, when and how.

This use of language and imposition of interventions further erodes and disorientates people from their mastery of their environments, the sense of who they are, their rich cultures and histories, skills and competencies. Thus these responses to poverty can contribute to communities losing further influence. Some communities that have succumbed to this view have lost it all. This phenomenon is extremely painful and hard to escape.

One of the most painful aspects of poverty is not having influence over one's environment (Damas & Rayhan, 2004). This lack of influence can make the difference between truly living and merely surviving. Narrative practice as social action/economic development builds on local initiatives, local actions and local knowledge.

This provides opportunities for individuals and communities not only to protect important aspects of life, but also to reclaim what they have lost, and learn new things to enrich their lives. (Caleb Wakhungu, personal communication, 29 May 2017)

The following extract explains the approach of the Mt Elgon Self-Help Community.

Raising our heads above the clouds[2]

The work of Caleb Wakhungu and the
Mt Elgon Self-Help Community

We have developed particular ways of using narrative practices to motivate social action. Even in circumstances of poverty, disease and hardship, communities have their own resources. Community members have their own histories, and their own knowledges and skills. They have their own hopes and dreams. We are using these existing resources. We are using our own histories in ways that inspire action.

This process begins when we call an initial meeting in a community and start to talk together. As facilitators, we start asking questions. These are questions that seek to learn about the resources of history in this particular place and at this particular time.

Step one: Sharing stories of pride and survival

During the first part of the meeting, we ask participants to share experiences. We particularly want to hear stories about what people are proud about in relation to their family, their community or their own lives. We ask each participant to tell us something that he or she has been able to do well. If they cannot think of something of which they are proud, we ask a different question: 'How have you been able to survive up until now? What have been some of the things you have been doing to survive?'

As people tell stories, we facilitators ask them more questions. We ask them for details, such as how they took particular steps, and about who was involved and so on. We ask them to give a name to the initiatives that they have been taking. We help them to name the different skills and the special knowledge that they have been using to survive. We do this to enrich the stories that people are telling.

Here is an example of the sort of story we hear in our first meetings:

Muyama is a widow taking care of six children. During our conversation, we asked her to share with us what she does to earn a living. She replied: 'When I lost my husband two years ago, I thought this was the end of the world for me and my children. We entirely depended on him for provision of basic needs and life was so bad for one year.'

When we asked her what she was doing in order to ensure the survival of her family, we learnt that she was carrying water to supply the restaurants in the Bumbo Trading Center. Muyama was carrying 20 jerry cans of 20 litres each per day. Through doing this hard physical work, she was earning just enough to buy food for her children. She also told us: 'I also wash clothes for people, especially those at the Bumbo Trading Center. And occasionally I sell cooked food and sugar cane. This is how our family is surviving at this time.'

Step two: Outsider-witness responses

Towards the end of the meeting, the Mt Elgon volunteers stand up and speak. We offer outsider-witness responses (M. White, 1995b, 2000, 2007). We speak about what we have heard in the stories that people have told, what was most significant to us, why this was significant and how these stories had affected us.

For example, after listening to Muyama we highlighted the following skills that we heard in her stories:

- her physical strength and endurance

- her skills in building good relationships with the people at the Bumbo Trading Center

- her skills in organisation, in order to be able to conduct all this work and still provide care for her children

- her good communication skills that make it possible for her to sell food to people in the market

- her agricultural skills and knowledge about sugar cane harvesting and selling.

We also reflected back what it meant to hear about her hard work and dedication to care for her children. We linked these to the stories of other women who were also in the meeting, and to the histories of mothers caring for children in Uganda through difficult times. We spoke of our respect for the work and dedication of mothers.

These retellings take place in a ceremonial way. We take care to honour the stories and initiatives that have been shared with us through songs and traditional dances.

Step three: Hopes and dreams

Having acknowledged the steps that each person has been taking, the initiatives they have been involved with in order to survive, we take care to name the contributions that each person has been making. We then ask a further question: 'What does this say about the dreams or hopes that you have for your future life?'

Participants then start to speak about their hopes and dreams for the future. These might be hopes for their own lives, or hopes for their families or community. These might include taking care of children, ensuring food security for their family, taking children to school, building a better house, reuniting with family members, initiating income-generating projects, and/or taking part in community work.

Muyama mentioned three dreams: to take good care of her children, to ensure food security for her family and to diversify the ways in which she could earn income.

Step four: The histories of people's hopes and dreams

Once people start to speak about their dreams for the future, we want to learn about the histories of these dreams. Where did these dreams come from? Who passed them on? This is a very important part of the process of 'raising someone's head above the clouds'. We seek to make it possible for people to link their current actions, and their hopes and dreams, to the legacies of those who have come before them. We consider ourselves to be the living legacies of those who have passed away.

When we asked Muyama about the histories that inform her dream of taking good care of her children, she linked this to her grandmother who took good care of Muyama and her sibling when her parents died. Muyama said that her grandmother would sometimes go without food, but that she made sure the children always had something to eat.

Muyama also connected her dream of ensuring food security for her family to her grandmother who used to work so hard to provide food. Muyama told us stories of how her grandmother would work in the garden from sunrise to sunset, only ever returning home to prepare food for the children before soon returning to her labours.

Muyama said that her dream of developing income-generating projects was connected to another mother in the village. This mother had separated from the father of her children and Muyama had admired the ways in which she fended for her family before she died. This woman had a poultry farm, five cows and vegetable gardens. She also knew how to grow maize. All these projects enabled her to earn income to support her family, and Muyama had been inspired by this.

This narrative process takes as its starting point the initiatives that people are already taking in their lives. No matter the hardships that people are experiencing, individuals and communities are always taking initiatives to try to respond to these hardships and to minimise the effects of such hardships on their lives and the lives of their loved ones. For instance, in response to her husband's death, Muyama had been carrying water, washing clothes and selling food in the marketplace. Implicit within these responses are certain skills, knowledge and values. Narrative practices are used to elicit and then richly acknowledge these skills and values through what are known as 'outsider-witness practices' (M. White, 1995b, 2000, 2007). The Mt Elgon volunteers noticed and acknowledged Muyama's particular skills in building good relationships, in organisation and communication, and her physical strength and endurance.

Through outsider-witness responses, her values of hard work and dedication to her children were linked to the storylines of other women who were present and to the history of women's work in these communities. These rich forms of acknowledgment and the rituals that contribute to the interlinking of people's stories involve song and traditional dance as well as words. This ceremonial process generates a sense of pride and dignity in participants. It also facilitates a sense of being connected to skills, to one another and to community histories. It enables people to experience themselves as knowledgeable and as active in the face of hard times.

After such acknowledgment of people's current initiatives and the skills and values implicit within them, it becomes more possible for people to speak of the future. Implicit within people's current actions, no matter how small these actions may be, are certain hopes or dreams for the future. When Muyama was asked about this, she spoke of a range of dreams for her children and herself: to take good care of her children, to ensure food security for her family and to diversify the ways in which she could earn income.

There is always a social history to people's dreams and wishes. By inviting people to speak about their hopes, and then by tracing the social history of these, a rich textual history is created. It is this process that we refer to as 'raising heads above the clouds'. This involves using the resources of people's stories and histories to spark possibilities for change.

The hopes that Muyama spoke about were soon interwoven with the legacies of her grandmother and other women in her village. In doing so, Muyama was assisted to define a broader purpose of her existence. Once this broader purpose was articulated and linked to significant histories in her life, it became much more possible for Muyama to consider further action.

Step five: Call to action

At this time, we then challenge participants to take an action: to come up with a particular assignment that will be the next step towards fulfilling their dreams. This can be done individually or in groups. It can be a small step or a large step.

Having realised that her grandmother and the mothers in the village were outstanding figures in her life, Muyama said she could not afford to sit back and wait as the family demands would only increase. She said that she realised that she needed to get started on something. She decided to join the women's saving group and to start a vegetable garden.

Our entire approach is built around making it possible for people to take action, and then ensuring that the action is sustainable.

Step six: Documenting the call to action

Participants are requested to write down the action that they have committed themselves to. In fact, if there is time, they often create a booklet around this particular theme. Each participant writes a small book explaining how they have overcome obstacles in the past, their dreams for the future, why this dream is important, where it has come from, and they describe the practical steps they will next put in place. Participants experience power over obstacles in their lives when they spend time writing these booklets, which remind them of their strengths, skills and knowledges.

Step seven: Circulating the documentation and generating excitement

The documents that are created are then read aloud to the assembled group, and participants and facilitators respond to them. These documents are also archived in our community library. People read these booklets and give comments and reflections back to their authors. These processes surround people's commitments with excitement. To create audiences and interest around people's commitments is one of our key tasks. We seek to get people interested in their own histories, their own dreams and their own actions.

As Muyama became interested in her own initiatives, her own histories, dreams and actions, this proved to be a significant turning point:

When I joined the Mt. Elgon women's group, I learnt skills in business management. We meet regularly to discuss various issues that include parenting, family planning, income generation, savings and loans, and initiating projects. It makes a difference to listen to each other's stories and offer each other help. At present, I have a garden of vegetables that I sell to buy food for my children and to support them with scholastic materials. I am now saving money with the group, and soon I will take a loan from the group in order to buy a cow that I hope will give me milk to sell and raise more income.

This is one of the processes we use to 'raise heads above the clouds'. It involves eliciting people's current initiatives, and richly acknowledging the skills and values involved in these. It involves linking these skills and actions to hopes and dreams, and then tracing the social history of these dreams. This process of moving backward and forward across time gradually builds a collective momentum.

Once it starts you cannot just stand by and watch! Everyone wants to get involved. It becomes possible to run without getting weary.

Culture, economics and narrative practice

The Mt Elgon Self-Help Community Project was the first to propose a form of collective narrative practice as social action and economic 'development'. The word 'development' is placed in inverted commas in acknowledgment of the ways in which the discourse of development as a cultural system is directly implicated in neocolonialism (Escobar, 1995; Esteva, 2010). The concept of development is all too often used in ways that imply majority world cultures and economies are inferior to those of the highly developed world and that the solution to such inferiority is to follow particular colonial blueprints or impositions that in turn threaten to lead to a reduction of local communities' autonomy, a decrease in cultural diversity and environmental destruction.

Amartya Sen (2004) has described how, generally speaking, 'economists pay inadequate attention to culture in investigating the operation of societies in general and the process of development in particular' (2004, p. 37). Where culture is discussed in development literature (Harrison & Huntington, 2000; Landes, 2000), too often the cultures of the majority world are described as somehow 'the enemy' – 'a voice from the past that inhibits societies from functioning in the modern world' (Rao & Walton, 2004, p. 10). On the other hand, it could also be said that those involved in community and collective responses to hardship, social suffering and/ or trauma pay inadequate attention to economics.

Wolfgang Sachs (2010) has argued that what is required is a 'decolonization of the imagination' (2010, p. ix), and that there can be 'no equity without ecology in the twenty-first century' (2010, p. xii). He suggests that rather than use the word development we can instead talk of 'post-development initiatives'. These act in favour of greater autonomy for communities and emphasise a transition from economies based on fossil-fuel resources to economies based on biodiversity. They oppose the trend to functionalise work, education and the land in order to boost economic efficiency, insisting on the right to act according to values of culture, democracy and justice. (Sachs, 2010, p. xiii).

The reason this broader context is relevant here is that the form of collective narrative practice proposed by the work of Caleb Wakhungu and the Mt Elgon Self-Help Community Project can be seen as an example of a 'post-development initiative'. This is a post-development initiative based on grassroots leadership and autonomy in which culture and history, far from being conceived of as the enemy, are gateways to social agency and possibility.

'Raising our heads above the clouds' provides a practical example congruent with the theory of Arjun Appadurai in his influential paper 'The capacity to aspire: Culture and the terms of recognition' (2004). In this paper, Appadurai focuses on one dimension of culture – 'its orientation to the future':

> In taking this approach to culture, we run against some deeply held counterconceptions. For more than a century, culture has been viewed as a matter of one or other kind of pastness – the keywords here are habit, custom, heritage, tradition. On the other hand, development is always seen in terms of the future – plans, hopes, goals, targets. This opposition is an artefact of our definitions and has been crippling. (Appadurai, 2004, p. 60)

The work of Caleb Wakhungu weaves between present, past and future, using people's stories of present and past survival to lift heads above the clouds in order to aspire to and take future action. Aspirations have a social history and creating rich textual heritage can enable people to look forward. The processes described in 'Raising our heads above the clouds' shape individual and collective horizons.

I am indebted to the work of Elspeth McAdam (McAdam, 1998; McAdam & Lang, 2010) in thinking more about the relationship between the past, present and future in collective narrative practice. Just as narrative practice emphasises multiple storylines of the past, Elspeth encourages the discussion of plural futures (personal communication, June 24, 2010). She invites community members to imagine not only talking with ancestors and considering what the ancestors may like to tell those of us in the present, but also to imagine talking to future generations: what we would like to tell them, and what they might like to ask us. Exploring ways to speak about the future in imaginative (non-linear) ways is a continuing challenge. In future projects perhaps we will consider the exchanging of messages between ancestors and generations to come.

Appadurai (2004) also describes the challenge of bringing 'the politics of dignity and the politics of poverty into a single framework' (2004, p. 63). He describes the significance of public and ceremonial moments in which the capacity to aspire is built by 'changing the terms of recognition' (2004, p. 77). A scintillating example of this is provided in 'Raising our heads above the clouds' when Caleb Wakhungu honours the achievements of young people at the public launch of a solar project:

We acknowledge the achievements of our young people. They may not have had shoes, enough clothes, and books to use at school, at times they may have gone without food, but they persisted through adversity to go on to higher institutions of learning and now they have done something that no-one else has done in our community. They have made our first solar panels. They have assembled these themselves. Over so many generations, our people have struggled to protect their crops from the heat of the sun and the strength of the winds. Their sacrifice has not been in vain. Now the dreams of our ancestors have come true. The hard work of our young people has made it possible for us to harness the heat of the sun. We acknowledge the achievements of our young people. It may have not been so easy for them along the way, but we are so happy that they raised their heads above the clouds. (Wakhungu in Denborough, 2010c, p. 20)

In this way, the achievements and aspirations of 'the future generation' are linked to the dreams of ancestors. Recognition is offered through the eyes of ancestry. Time and again in the work of the Mt Elgon Self-Help Community Project, the 'politics of recognition' are connected to 'the politics of material life' (Appadurai, 2004, p. 80).

If culture is a 'dialogue between aspirations and sedimented traditions' (Appadurai, 2004, p. 84), then as practitioners it is our task to find ways for this dialogue to spark and sustain meaningful social action. This task is at the heart of the collective narrative practice at Mt Elgon.

Diverse economic 'development' – different kinds of economic beings and relationship

Having described the ways in which the work of the Mt Elgon Self-Help Community Project represents a post-development initiative in which local culture is utilised as a gateway to social agency and possibility, and having considered the ways in which Caleb Wakhungu is enhancing the capacity to aspire by linking a politics of recognition with a politics of material life, I now wish to propose that the work at Mt Elgon provides an example of diverse economic practice, which in turn enables different kinds of economic beings and relationships.

> The political, ethical, social, philosophical problem of our day is not to try to liberate the individual from the economy ... but to liberate us both from the economy and from the type of individualization that is linked to the economy. We have to promote new forms of subjectivity through the refusal of this kind of individuality which has been imposed on us for several centuries. (Foucault, 1983, p. 216)

In my observation, the model provided by the Mt Elgon Self-Help Community Project offers the possibility of invigorating a 'new economic politics' (Gibson-Graham, 2006, p. xxxiv). Feminist economists Katherine Gibson and Julie Graham (who publish as J. K. Gibson-Graham) emphasise the significance of making 'visible the hidden and alternative economic activities that everywhere abound' (Gibson-Graham, 2006, p. xxiv), and in doing so constructing a language of the 'diverse economy ... populated by various capitalist and noncapitalist institutions and practices' (2006, p. 54). Their work is an attempt to expand our 'economic vocabulary' (2006, p. 62) to include different kinds of transaction, different types of labour and different forms of enterprise (2006, pp. 62–63). In doing so, they hope to bring forth 'new ethical practices of thinking economy', which in turn can enable 'different kinds of economic beings' (2006, p. xxvii).

The work of the Mt Elgon Self-Help Community Project has been sparking and sustaining diverse economic 'projects'. It has prioritised not only market-based economic activity, but, through the principle of 'the gift of giving' and a range of collective narrative practices that link individual action to a collective ethos and collective action (savings clubs, collective house-building processes), it equally prioritises what are sometimes referred to as 'informal economies' (Gibson-Graham, 2006, p. 58) or 'non-market economies' (2006, p. 26). At the same time, the work at Mt Elgon has prioritised environmentally sustainable economies and biodiversity. This work therefore represents the use of collective narrative practices to spark and sustain three interrelating strands of diverse economics: market-based economic activity, non-market transactions and relations, and environmental and economic transformation.

This is not the place for a full diverse economic accounting of the Mt Elgon Self-Help Community Project, but I do wish to draw attention to the significance of diverse economic practice and how it influences forms of subjectivity. In writing about a slum dwellers' alliance in Mumbai, Gibson and Graham (Gibson-Graham, 2006) describe the ways in which certain forms of economic practice are linked to new practices of self:

> Saving groups are the consciousness-raising groups of the Alliance ... It is in these small groups that individuals embark on a project of ethical self-transformation in Foucault's ... terms, or a micropolitics of (re)subjectivation in Connolly's terms ... To join such a group is to engage in new practices of the self – setting aside savings

from what is already too little to live on in the case of the women slum dwellers ... In the process, new senses of self are instituted – through self-developments as citizens, house designers, investors, or entrepreneurs, through self-recognition of their survival capacities as poor women and migrants, through daily recommitment to the cultivation of solidarity. The savings groups focused on individual self-transformation are the foundation on which alternative economic interventions are built. (Gibson-Graham, 2006, p. xxv)

Similarly, the work of Mt Elgon Self-Help Community Project involves 'new' practices of self, but these are sparked and sustained by interweaving present hopes and dreams with the perspectives and views of the ancestors. What is new is also old.

Narrative practice as social action: Definitional ceremonies come full circle

In considering the work of the Mt Elgon Self-Help Community Project as an example of narrative practice as social action, it seems relevant to explore the histories of the links between narrative practice and social action. These histories can be traced back to the work of anthropologist Barbara Myerhoff (1982) and her concept of 'definitional ceremony'. Barbara Myerhoff coined the term definitional ceremony to describe particular rituals through which members of an elderly Jewish community in Venice Beach actively defined their collective identity:

Socially marginalized people. Disdained, ignored groups. Individuals with what Erving Goffman calls 'spoiled identities', regularly seek opportunities to appear before others in the light of their own internally provided interpretation ... I have called such performances 'Definitional ceremonies', understanding them to be collective self-definitions specifically intended to proclaim an interpretation to an audience not otherwise available. (Myerhoff, 1982, p. 105)

Two of the definitional ceremonies that Myerhoff (1986) described in detail involved collective social action: a protest march and a public mural depicting the political and social history of the community. Their intent was to alter 'more than their own version of themselves' (Myerhoff, 1986, p. 267) and to bring about wider changes in meaning, understanding and social practice. These ceremonies were forms of social action and Myerhoff's descriptions of them invite us to remember that identity formation and social action are not separate. Convening definitional ceremonies in relation to various initiatives of social action that people are taking can powerfully influence not only these people's self-definition, but also their ability to continue to take action.

One of the aims of collective narrative practice is to find ways to convene ceremonies in which people act as outsider witnesses and as engaged participants joined in social projects for a broader good (see Denborough, 2008), an aim that has come to fruition in the work of the Mt Elgon Self-Help Community Project.

Michael White was introduced to the work of Barbara Myerhoff by David Epston, and he then proceeded to reorientate his work towards the creation of narrative therapy as definitional ceremony (M. White, 1995b, 1999). He often referred to outsider-witness practice and definitional ceremonies as the most powerful forms of therapeutic practice he had ever participated in (M. White, 2007, p. 218). The concept of definitional ceremony also provided a bridge between narrative therapeutic practice and narrative community gatherings (M. White, 2003).

In the work of Mt Elgon, we see the concept of definitional ceremony and outsider-witness work turn full circle. In the 1980s, Barbara Myerhoff (1982, 1986) developed the concept in fieldwork within a community of elderly Jews in Venice Beach. This concept was then taken into narrative therapeutic practice and honed by Michael White (1995b, 2000, 2007). Now Caleb Wakhungu is using these ideas, concepts and practices within a community context to enable stories of pride and survival, and the personal, social and cultural histories of these stories, to be harnessed in order to raise heads above the clouds, to build the capacity to aspire, and to engage in social actions in realms of economy diversity.

What is unique about the work of the Mt Elgon Self-Help Community Project is the way in which it engages narrative practices to spark and sustain diverse economies. It is, to my knowledge, the first project of its kind.

Notes

1. Caleb Wakhungu can be contacted via wcaleb2003@yahoo.co.uk
2. This extract is from Denborough (2010c).

Chapter 7

'Gathering up courage':
Can narrative practice play a part in sustaining
activism and human rights work?

Can narrative practices play a part in sustaining activism and human rights work? Can this be done in ways that avoid depoliticising experience and contribute to sustaining broader social movement rather than undermining it? These seem important questions and they are the focus of this chapter.

There is a longstanding critique of the ways in which individualising therapeutic practices can inadvertently undermine social movements (Kitzinger & Perkins, 1993; Pupavac, 2001, 2002a, 2002b, 2006). In recent years, the concept of 'burnout', and accompanying proposals for 'self-care' as an antidote, have become pervasive, so much so that these phrases are now heard not only within activist circles in Western countries but also in human rights organisations and social movements in countries far from where these concepts were first developed and distributed.

Vikki Reynolds (2011) has written about the hazards of an individualised and psychologised concept of burnout:

I don't think as therapists and community workers we're burning out. The problem of burnout is not in our heads or in our hearts, but in the real world where there is a lack of justice. (Reynolds, 2011, p. 28)

She has also proposed the importance of fostering collective sustainability and collective care (in contrast to self-care):

We promote sustainability in relationships with each other, not as a series of isolated, individual projects. I am interested in our collective care, and our collective sustainability, which is reciprocal, communal and inextricably linked with spirited practices of solidarity. (Reynolds, 2011, p. 32)

I share Bharati Acharya's (2010) determination to develop ways in which narrative practices can support those who work tirelessly for social change:

Through the practices of illuminating the complicated and multi-layered nature of the work of social activists, I believe narrative methods acknowledge the arduous realities they face without expunging their very real experiences of optimism, reward, and joy. Furthermore, narrative methods of 'rescuing the said from the saying of it' (Newman, 2008) can play a vital role in creating living reservoirs of valuable knowledge that can serve to inspire and sustain both present and future workers for social change. (Acharya, 2010, pp. 38–39)

This chapter presents a number of narrative methodologies and explores how these can foster collective sustainability.

An invitation from the International Women's Development Agency

The work described below was inspired by an invitation from the International Women's Development Agency and in particular by Manon van Zuijlen.[1] It was Manon who approached Dulwich Centre Foundation in 2013 to co-facilitate workshops with her in Chiang Mai and Mae Sot, Thailand. Manon and IWDA have longstanding partnerships with a number of women's organisations that represent different ethnic minorities from Myanmar and respond to human rights violations. The participants in the proposed workshops were to be women working for gender justice and self-determination for their people in profoundly difficult contexts.[2]

Manon hoped that these workshops would have two purposes. First, to share existing narrative ways of working and co-develop with participants new culturally resonant methods that could then be used by participants to respond to women in Myanmar who were struggling with the effects of human rights abuses. And second, to enable the workers, who themselves were facing many obstacles, to tell their stories in ways that would sustain them and their work.

The following pages describe how collective narrative timelines, maps of history, collective documents and definitional ceremonies were used in these workshops to foster collective sustainability. The perspectives, stories, sparkling ideas and proposals of the activists and human rights workers from Myanmar are woven throughout.

Particular ways of engaging with history: Collective timelines and maps of history

At the beginning of each workshop, we created collective timelines and maps of women's history. These are particular ways of engaging with history. They are inspired by the work of Highlander Folk School (now Highlander Research and Education Center), which has been described as a social movement 'half-way house' (Morris, 1984, p. 139).

We were first introduced to the use of collective timelines through the Highlander Research and Education Center, where they have been used as a methodology of popular education for many years. Historically, workers at Highlander invited participants in workshops to speak about their 'Seeds of fire' (see Adams & Horton, 1975; Horton, J. Kohl, & H. Kohl, 1998; Jacobs, 2003). These were the moments in the participants' lives when the spark to contribute to broader social change first occurred. People were invited to name the date this occurred, to write this and a short story associated with the particular event on a card, and then place this on a broader collective timeline that had been mapped out around the room where the workshop was taking place. Often, a parallel timeline was also spoken about and depicted, this being the broader timeline of whatever issue people were meeting together to try to address. For instance, if the group was meeting in relation to labour relations, then a history of the labour movement might be depicted on one timeline, while the collective timeline created from participants' stories would run parallel to this around the room ... In the mid-1990s, Cheryl White visited Highlander outside Knoxville, Tennessee, and was so impressed with the effectiveness of collective timelines that she encouraged me and others to explore their use in our work contexts. (Denborough, 2008, p. 144)

The following extended extract describes, in the words of participants, how narrative practices 'unearthed hidden histories that give us strength'.[3]

Unearthing hidden histories that give us strength: Collective timelines and maps of women's history

When we are working for women, when we are working for gender justice, and when we are facing many obstacles, it can be significant to bring our histories with us. In particular, it can be significant to talk about and document women's histories that can give us strength.

Together, we created collective timelines and maps of women's history (Denborough, 2008). In pairs, we interviewed each other, asking the following questions:

1. What date did you start working for/with women?

2. At this time, what was drawing you or driving you to work with women? Was it a particular hope, commitment, dream or value? Please come up with a name for this theme. Examples might include 'Making a big noise about violence', 'To help my neighbours', 'Justice'.

3. What is the history of this hope, commitment, dream or value? What date did this come into your life? This will be an earlier date than the one listed in #1. Please name the earliest date that you can connect your theme to. This could even be a date prior to your birth if you consider your actions to be carrying on the efforts of other women who came before you. What is the story that explains your passion to work for women?

4. Who would be least surprised to know that this is important to you?

5. When you think of this theme, what is drawing you to work with women, what image comes to mind? What picture could we include on the timeline to symbolise this?

Each woman then listed the date she started working for women on the lower timeline (see picture). She then listed the name of her theme and its date on the upper timeline and retold their story to the group. While the women were speaking, the facilitators 'rescued' their words and turned these into documents which are included below.

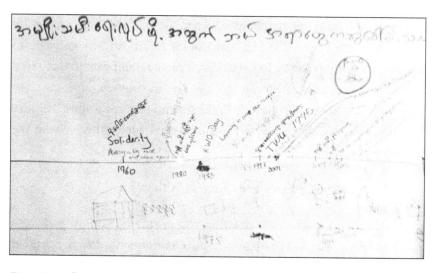

Figure 16. A collective narrative timeline

During this process, the facilitators asked about other significant dates and other significant women who could be placed on the timeline. These included the dates that key women's organisations were formed, women chiefs of particular villages, and women who had made significant cultural contributions. International Women's Day was also acknowledged. In this way, the timeline came to represent both personal and collective women's history.

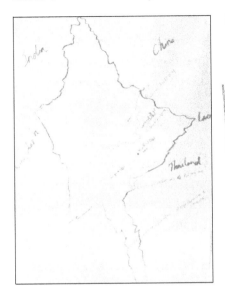

Figure 17. Map of women's history

Map of women's history

Each woman was also asked to name where this hope, commitment, dream or value came from, what place?

Each of these places, and each woman's theme, was then marked on a map of history. Some women's stories involved significant journeys and these were also honoured on this map.

Rescuing words and creating collective documents

While the women were sharing key histories through the timeline and the map, the facilitators had been granted permission to rescue the words in order to craft collective documents. The following document was created from this process.

Candlelight in the dark: A hidden history that gives us strength

This morning we met together. At first there was thunder and then there was conversation. Together, we created a timeline of women's history. We come from different places, different people. We have different languages and songs. But we are all working for our people, for our women. We are working for an end to violence, for gender equality, for education. We are working for the daughters who never come home.

For some of us, we started with questions. As a child, I would sit in the classroom and think, 'Why can't I learn in my own language?' As a young woman, I would ask myself 'How can I help my neighbours?' We carried these questions for many years, just waiting, looking for a chance to take action. Now we are taking action.

We carry with us our mothers' stories and stories from older women. When I went to study in the city I wrote a letter home to my mother. But she could not read it. My father had to read my words to her. From that moment on, I have been determined to fight for women's education. My mother supports me in this work. She did not prohibit me. She knows I am working for my people, for women.

Some of us work to stop violence because violence was in our homes. When we were children we could not stop it. People would say, 'Men have always been doing this', but our eyes were opened. How have we kept going? Some of it is personal determination. Some of it is knowing there are other women's groups which are also taking action. And some of it is the support we have gained from the Women's League of Burma. Now there is no turning back.

We have learnt so much along the way. Some of us have been on a quest for education. This started with my parents. There were no educated people in my village in the jungle, but my parents knew it was important so they sent me to school in the city, with Burmans. I was the only one from an ethnic minority. I had very long hair, traditional clothes and a rural accent. They would push me off the edge of the long bench at lunch time, but it did not stop me seeking education. Nothing has stopped me in this quest. It is a quest that has travelled thousands of miles. My path of learning is now marked on our map of history.

Another member of our group said: It was when I left high school that my eyes were opened. I started to learn about the daughters who leave our villages and never come home. Their parents expect to see them at the special festivals but they never come. Only later did I learn that these daughters have been trafficked to China, sometimes sold and sold again and sold again; so vulnerable to abuse, so unjust. And yet it has become normal. It is not normal to us. Our eyes are open and we seek justice.

When I was 14 years old there was a domestic worker from a jungle village who lived in my community. She was raped by the son in the household. He violated her and then refused to marry her. This woman reported this to the head of the community. She tried to seek justice in so many ways. Every time she was knocked back she kept trying; one way, then another way, until finally she left our community. But I have never forgotten her and the way she struggled for justice. Now I am carrying on this struggle. If she knew about this, I think she would support me. I think she would be satisfied that her efforts for justice inspired a fourteen-year-old girl. I will never forget her.

We are all working for women and our histories push us forward. I remember in 2000, soldiers came into our village. These were local soldiers. There were no men in our house at that time, just my mother, my aunt and a guest. It was night and we were outside around the fire when we heard a local soldier hitting his wife. We heard her run away, not far from us. And then we heard the soldier in his military boots running towards our place. We quickly put out the fire so he could not use its light to find his wife and we ran into the house. This made the soldier very angry. He held his gun at us and said we must rebuild the fire. I was very scared. I did not dare to look at his face. But we did not relight the fire. Instead we stood together and shouted very loudly. When the other community soldiers heard us they shot their guns into the air. The soldier with us was frightened and he ran away. Some of us, for a long time, have been making a loud noise to stop violence.

These are our stories. This is our history. It is personal history and it is also women's history. On our timeline, we have included the dates when our organisations were founded. We have included the fact that since the 1980s, many Karen villages have had women as their chiefs. When all the men had to flee from the Burmese military, Karen women remained and took charge. And we have included some of the women we most admire, including a songwriter who wrote songs that all Palaung people could understand. She sings for love and for country. She sings for us and has done so much for our people. And we have included the first time that we celebrated International Women's Day in Burma/Myanmar.

Definitional ceremonies as solidarity and sustenance

There was an element of enactment and ritual involved in this process that is more difficult to convey on paper. With the timeline and map placed up on the wall of the building we were meeting in, each participant spoke to particular histories and publicly inscribed these in front of witnesses.

Figure 18. Retelling histories

When the collective documents were read aloud (in two languages) there was a reverence and honouring of each other's interwoven contributions. It is possible to understand these rituals as definitional ceremonies (Myerhoff, 1982, 1986; M. White, 1995b, 1999). In this context, these ceremonies were creating a particular sort of solidarity and collective sustenance.

What this process made possible

After the creation of the timelines, maps of women's history and collective documents, the women spoke about what it had meant to them to speak about and document what they called the 'hidden histories' of their values and commitments:

This is very energising. We are not paid well and our work is difficult. Sometimes we want to give up. But this helps us to go on. It reassures us about what we are doing.

Linking the women's current actions and initiatives with the histories of what they give value to (including treasured people and places) and then interweaving individual storylines into collective tapestries, such as timelines, maps and documents, contributed to the creation of a 'usable past' (Wertsch, 2002, p. 45): a history that can spur current and future actions. Once a rich 'textual heritage' (Lowenthal, 1994, p. 53) and a shared heritage of achievement has been acknowledged, it can become easier to look towards the future.

We only do the work, we don't see how important it is; it is good to be reminded.

Rescuing the women's words and stories, and retelling these in the form of documents, timelines and maps, made visible and acknowledged what often goes unseen: women's actions and achievements.

Despite all the difficulties, we have accomplished a lot!

Because the two documents were 'double-storied' (Denborough, 2008), they acknowledged hardships faced, but particularly emphasised women's acts of resistance and the significance of these.

Before today, we never knew why each other was here. We are often together and we work together, but we did not know what reasons had brought us to this work.

Enabling participants to introduce themselves through the histories of what is important to them, and enabling women to tell rich historical accounts of what they give value to, made it much more likely that the women's stories would resonate with one another. The process also made it possible for participants to recognise and authenticate each other's activism and why they were engaged in it.

It can be difficult to see each other's roles. Sometimes we fail to recognise each other's contributions to this work. This timeline makes it clear that everyone's work is important.

The process of collectively and ritually recognising each participant's theme and history enabled an 'invention of unity in diversity' (Freire, 1994, p. 157) and the establishment of 'communitas' (Turner, 1969, 1979), a sense of togetherness in which differences and individual distinctiveness remain visible and treasured. This seems particularly relevant when bringing together participants from diverse organisations and ethnic groups.

How we can use timelines and maps of history in our work

Significantly, participants then spoke of different ways in which they could use timelines and maps of women's history in their continuing work.

Strategic planning

These are confusing times with differences between organisations inside and outside of Burma/Myanmar. We can use this for strategy planning. We can look back at what has been achieved and then we can look forward.

Safe houses

Some of us work in women's safe houses. We could create a timeline on which we mark different women's skills ... This was the date when I first sought safety ... This was the date I learnt about trust or women standing together ... When women come into the safe house they could see other women's themes and stories. And when the time is right they could add their own.

With individual women

I wonder if we could create timelines for individual women too?

Sharing documents

We can share the documents of our hidden histories with others in our organisation. And with other women.

'Gathering up courage' through richly describing survival skills

As an alternative to introducing practices of 'self-care', the second part of this workshop focused on listening for and documenting women's survival skills and then convening definitional ceremonies in relation to this. Informed by considerations of double-storied testimony (Denborough, 2005), participants were invited to interview each other and document each other's 'survival skills' – the ways in which they had endured hardships. It was hoped that this would serve two purposes. First, that it would introduce the notion of 'double-listening': ways of listening for and acknowledging not only the injustices and effects of human rights abuses, but also the second story of women's survival and responses to injustice. Second, it was hoped this process would make visible participants' own insider knowledges of enduring hardship. Documenting and sharing survival stories among activists and human rights workers can foster collective sustainability and collective care (Reynolds, 2011) and broaden the available repertoire of ways of sustaining themselves and each other.

Significantly, the document we produced in the workshop weaves between individual and collective voice. It begins with these words:

> Burmese women have had to develop so many different skills in survival. We are smart in survival skills. When I think about this, I think of my mother. Time and again she had to move us, her children. My father is fighting for our state and my mother would gather us together and we would move. We would start again, often living under only something to keep off the rain. She would raise chickens for our food. She would cook even in the rain. She would make shelter and try to keep our spirits up. I have never thought about this before, but my mother has so many survival skills. I want to talk to her about this. Other Burmese women have had to survive in displaced persons camps and refugee camps. Some of us have had to survive men's violence. And we have had to create new lives in a different country. Burmese women, our sisters, are smart in survival. And now, as we continue to work for the rights of women, we too call upon skills in getting through hard times.

A diversity of survival skills were spoken. They included: 'to look at the face of my child', 'to rest and sleep', 'crying and tears', 'music, song and karaoke', 'thinking of good memories', 'working hard even if we just want to go home' and 'writing through hard times'. These were not 'self-care' strategies imported from elsewhere, these were local survival skills with rich histories. Each survival skill or theme was storied, historicised and linked to others. Here are two examples. The first is from an older woman, the second is from one of the younger participants.

To protect ourselves

Some of us have had to learn how to protect ourselves. When I was growing up, my parents prohibited me from going anywhere. They were afraid that I could be raped or gossiped about by other people. I didn't agree. I was angry and so I tried to find a way to protect myself. I learnt martial arts. Even though my father didn't like this, I continued and I got a black belt. Then my father got really, really angry at me. He challenged men in the community to try to rape me. Some people dared to come and, as I had a black belt, so they learned the consequences. Now I use my skills in martial arts in art shows and in traditional ceremonies. And they help me to not accept what other people say, to not accept the restrictions that other people try to place on my life. I do not accept it. Some of us have learnt to protect ourselves and to not accept the restrictions of others.

Gathering my courage: If I try hard enough everything is possible

Our work takes courage. And we know a lot about travelling through hard times. Some of us keep telling ourselves that everything is possible. I came to Mae Sot in 2013 because of my work. I had never travelled very far away before and I was not very sure how to get here. I was very worried that I would be tricked by other people, but I gathered all my strength, I held my courage around me, and I took the first step. I had to ride a car, and then another, and then another, and then another, and then another from northern Shan state to Mae Sot. Each time I was worried they might charge me more because I didn't know the place. But I kept gathering my courage around me. And I kept telling myself anything is possible. If I try hard enough anything is possible. Finally, I arrived in Mae Sot. Believing that anything is possible comes from my father. He wanted to become a doctor but did not graduate from high school.

Even without schooling he learnt about medicine from a military doctor for three years and now he knows how to treat other people. My father would not be surprised that I can gather my courage in this way. There is also a saying, 'If you try you could also become a Buddha'. Some of us, as we work for gender justice, we gather our courage around us and we remind ourselves that everything is possible.

The document closed in collective voice:

Burmese women have had to develop so many different skills in survival. Some of these skills have been passed down the generations. We are smart in survival. When we think about this, we think of our mothers, our sisters, our colleagues and ourselves.

What this process made possible

After these documents were 'performed' or read in two languages through further informal definitional ceremonies, the women spoke about what this process had meant to them:

Gathering up courage

This process was like gathering up courage.

Hearing my story read back has increased my sense of bravery. We will be more confident now in our skills.

Renewed sense of agency

Sometimes we don't have any control over the problem, but we do have power in relation to our survival skills. This gives us the power to overcome problems in the future.

Bringing 'secret' knowledge to light

I was very happy to hear my words. They were like a secret ... but now we write it out ... they appear. This makes me feel light.

A new relationship to the past

At the time of my difficulties, I just did what I had to do. I never thought about it. But this activity has helped me to analyse past experiences. I realise now that some of the things I did, even though they were very little, were solutions. They were survival skills.

Facing the future

This has made me feel strong. Remembering what I have been through means that in the future we will be able to overcome.

Shared experience

Listening to each other's stories is like watching a movie. We can learn from each other's stories. We may have our own ingredients, our own skills, but this way we can learn from others. I wish I was a film director: I would make a film out of everyone's stories!

Sustaining activists and action

This chapter has described how collective timelines, maps of history, collective documents and definitional ceremonies can be used to sustain the critical work of activists and human rights workers. These approaches seek to foster collective sustainability and collective care (Reynolds, 2011). They seek to enable solidarity and to re-engage with histories in ways that enable future action. Significantly, they seek to sustain activists and action.

Each of these methods aim to unearth, honour, richly describe and perform histories of the hopes, commitments, dreams and values that inspire action. In this way, they generate a 'textual heritage' to sustain these actions into the future. What's more, by linking the efforts of women in the present to those who initially inspired their social actions, and by linking individual women's actions to the actions of organisations, isolation was dissolved and agency sustained. At the same time, by highlighting the women's accomplishments, a heritage of achievement was generated, which stood in contrast to despair. Through this narrative process, not only were women activists sustained, but so too were their actions and the social movement for gender justice that they represent.

Attention to sustaining activists and action together was also relevant in enabling the women to speak about the skills they were using in their work towards gender justice. The survival skills that had assisted women to endure significant hardships included the following two disparate themes:

To rest and sleep

Sometimes, rest can be important. One of us said, 'I am very impatient and find it easy to get angry. I am aware that if I do not go away and rest, the problem will get bigger. So in hard times, I run away from the problem first, calm down, rest, think and find another way to solve the problem.' Others spoke of the significance of sleep. In times of hardship, sleep can be precious.

Working hard even if we just want to go home

Sometimes, even though we just want to go home, we know we must work harder. Ten years ago I was attending a Karen young women's leadership school. All the subjects were taught in Karen, but even though I am Karen, I didn't speak the language. I missed home very much, but I worked so hard to learn Karen language, very hard. And by the time I graduated I knew our language. This took strength and I learnt this from one of my friends' mothers. People who know me and my family would not be surprised that I am strong and that I work hard.

While 'working hard even if we just want to go home' is not often recommended within Western self-care strategies, it was named as a significant theme by women activists from Burma/Myanmar alongside the preciousness of sleep, 'looking at the face of my child', and many others. Not separating work from notions of self-care and collective care seems significant as we seek to sustain not only activists but also action.

It seems appropriate to close with words from the women from Burma/Myanmar:

'This process was like gathering up courage.'

Acknowledgments

The work described in this chapter was made possible due to the International Women's Development Agency and the support of AusAid's Australian NGO Cooperation Program (which provided funding), the Shan Women's Action Network, and in particular Kham Yard and Hseng Noung, Women's League of Burma, and Ying Lao for interpretation and cultural consultation.

Notes

1. Manon van Zuijlen organised the workshops in her role with IWDA. The workshops were facilitated by Cheryl White and David Denborough from Dulwich Centre Foundation and Manon van Zuijlen. Photographs by Manon van Zuijlen and David Denborough.

2. Representatives from the following organisations were involved: Shan Women's Action Network, Women's League of Burma, Palaung Women's Organisation, Karen Women's Organisation, Kachin Women's Association – Thailand, Burmese Women's Union, Lahu Women's Organisation, and Tavoyan Women's Union.

3. The text in the following section is an extract from the publication, *Narrative responses to human rights abuses: Sustaining women workers and honouring the survival skills of women from Burma/Myanmar* (Dulwich Centre Foundation International and International Women's Development Agency, 2013).

Chapter 8

Narrative practice
and social movement

In this chapter, I wish to explore how collective testimonies and other narrative methodologies are being used to support social movements and community organising. At the same time, I want to link these developments with writings by social movement theorists and community organisers who are engaging with the narrative metaphor. It's still early days in these explorations.

A significant proportion of this chapter relates to the work of Tineke Rumkabu, Danny Rayar, Ronny Kareni and Jason MacLeod and their dedication to a free West Papua. I would like to acknowledge their contributions at the outset.

Collective testimonies

In 2013, a citizens tribunal was conducted to coincide with the fifteenth anniversary of the Biak Massacre – a devastating event for West Papuans in which more than one hundred civilians were killed, raped or tortured.[1] This citizens tribunal looked and acted much like a court and followed the format of a coronial inquest (a formal inquiry into a death). While it had no formal jurisdiction, this tribunal was an action pursued by the long-running West Papuan independence movement and it received significant media coverage.[2]

West Papuan cultural practices and collective narrative practice informed the ways in which testimonies were told during this tribunal. The tribunal opened and closed with West Papuan song.[3] A number of testimonies were given individually and a collective testimony was also delivered. It is this collective testimony that I wish to discuss in this chapter as, some years on, it continues to reverberate and to be put to use by the West Papuan independence movement. The ways in which this has occurred seem to offer possibilities as to how collective narrative practices may be able to contribute in modest ways to supporting social movements.

About the collective testimony

The collective testimony is multi-voiced and multi-storied (see Denborough, 2005). Like the traditional mats that people from across the Pacific sit on, sleep on and conduct ceremony with, the testimony is woven from diverse strands: voices and vignettes from West Papuans who were consulted by Tineke Rumkabu, Danny Rayar, Ronny Kareni, Jason MacLeod, Aunty Barbara Wingard, David Newman and me, combined with the words of those Jason MacLeod had interviewed over 14 years (see MacLeod, 2015).[4]

As you will read below, this collective testimony has multiple themes:

- testimonies of injustice

- the effects of these injustices

- testimonies of remembrance

- stories of resistance, action and rescue

- Papuan survival skills

- hopes and dreams.

The version of the collective testimony first developed for the citizens tribunal focused specifically on the experience of the Biak Massacre. The current version, included below, has become a testimony that speaks on behalf of a diverse West Papuan citizenry with a common dream.

After sharing the testimony, I will discuss how it has been used by West Papuans and those supporting their struggle, and the possibilities this may offer others.

We have come to testify[5]

We have come to testify. There is much that we want the world to know.

We want you to travel with us to the remote places of Papua – Wamena, Paniai, the Jayawijaya Highlands, the Star Mountains, Mindiptana, Timika, Arso, Mamberamo, Biak, Merauke, Asmat and many other places. We want you to hear stories of suffering from the mouths of ordinary people. Our memories are clear and sharp.

'In this river our father was murdered.'

'On that mountain slope there used to be villages. They were destroyed by the military.'

'On that open field, our old men were forced to burn their koteka [penis sheaths] because they were considered primitive.'

'In the past that mountain was ours, now people have destroyed our mother.'

We want you to travel with us to the sites of the massacres. We want to testify about the killings and the beatings with rifles.

We want to testify about the people who were disappeared, those who were imprisoned and those who were tortured.

There have been many forms of torture – the burning, the stabbing of the genitals, the rape of women.

These are some of the injustices that we want the world to know.

On some days, bombs have fallen like rain. We have been up against Hercules aircraft and helicopters and boats. They had overwhelming power.

And after the massacres or murders, the injustices always continue.

Rather than acknowledge the truth, they tell lies.

The perpetrators are promoted not punished, while the victims are dragged into court.

Some of us have spent years in prison. One of us was jailed for 15 years simply for raising our Morning Star flag.

Over years we have faced one injustice after another and then another. There has been violation after violation since 1963. Entire villages have been destroyed. And Papuan people have been turned against other Papuans.

Injustices continue to this day. Today we face human rights violations, economic injustice, and every week thousands more migrants come in white ships and planes. We are becoming a minority in our land.

Those who resist face continuing discrimination. We are excluded from employment, education and health care. And for women, it has been worse. They suffered the rapes and assaults and then even more. They were shamed by their own families and often marriages broke apart. These are forms of double injustice and women's suffering that no-one should ever have to face.

These are just some of the injustices that we are testifying to today. We want the world to know about this.

We also want to testify to the effects of these injustices

Some of our bodies bear the scars.

And so do our souls. We will never forget the sound of the killings. Some of us still feel the fear. Those of us who fled don't know if we will be safe when we return.

Other survivors have been left with physical disabilities and troubles in the mind.

The rapes brought shame – so much shame that some women did not seek medical help.

And sometimes survivors may feel guilty for being alive. The killings can make us doubt that we have a right to live.

There have been effects for children too. Fear came to the children who did not go to school for months.

When the foreigners have taken our land, cut down our forests and destroyed our rivers, this destruction of our land affects us too. The loss of our sacred places has brought sickness to our people.

And sometimes we feel like we are slaves in our own land. Some of us have to struggle everyday just to feed our families and send our children to school.

But there is more that we want you to know.

We want you to know our testimonies of remembrance

We are survivors and also witnesses. We have always remembered those who were killed. We will remember them until we die.

There are many ways that we do this.

We have cultural ways of joining in memory and in prayer. We place stones or wreaths of flowers. And there are traditional songs that we use to connect us with those who have died and with the ancestors. These are songs we can sing to those who have passed. We do this in a quiet place: a garden, a beach.

Or we remember through making statues of our loved ones, or photos, or lighting candles. We commune with our ancestors.

But we never forget them. They are with us. Those of us who are still alive have a responsibility to keep progressing the struggle. I have dreams of those who were killed in the jungle. They come to me in my dreams and they encourage me to keep going. I dreamed of them just last week. I listen to their voices.

If they knew that we were meeting together now, if they knew that we were gathering this testimony, they would be very happy. This would mean something to them.

They have gone over there to another world. We will always remember them.

We also want you to know the stories of our resistance, action and rescue

Our people have a long, long history of resistance. We Papuans have been resisting outsiders for centuries. Back to the 1850s, the Dutch who were seeking to protect their spice trade faced more than 40 Papuan rebellions – both violent and nonviolent. Diverse tribes came together to resist. Angganeta Menufandu, a Konor (indigenous prophet) from Biak Island, led a mass defiance of government and mission bans on wor (ritual singing and dancing) and urged her followers not to pay taxes and to withhold labour. When the Japanese invaded, towards the end of World War II, they were initially welcomed, but, after their acts of cruelty, the movement for a free and independent West Papua began again. The killings and massacres began in these times. And our resistance continued.

Our struggle for freedom continued after WWII when the US drove the Japanese out of West Papua at the cost of thousands of lives. And since 1961 we have resisted Indonesian rule.

We remember our long history of resistance. This history raises us up. We carry it on.

Many of us have formed organisations of action. We come together for survivors of human rights abuses, for women, for people all over Papua. We form resistance groups. We are students, young people, older people, women, men, religious leaders and traditional leaders. We take action on behalf of those who are living and those who are no longer alive.

Some of us who witnessed massacres were involved in acts of rescue on the days when bullets were raining down, and when the sky was on fire. After the Biak Massacre our family gave shelter to two men who were fleeing for their lives. My father gave them his clothes and sat my sisters on their laps. We sat down quietly and we opened all the doors and all the windows. When the soldiers came in all their weaponry, we stood there shaking. As they held their guns at us, and asked us if we were hiding anyone, we said no. We were all shaking, my father, my sisters, myself, but we survived, and the two men survived too. For four days they stayed with us. We had almost no food but my mother found a way to feed us. We are survivors, rescuers and resisters.

Right across Papua, and for so many years, we have continued to resist, to rescue and to raise the Morning Star. When we could not fly our flag we have painted it on our bodies, stitched it into noken string bags. When one of us was imprisoned for 15 years for raising our flag, he was offered amnesty if he apologised, but he refused. 'Why should I say sorry? I have done nothing wrong. It is the Indonesian state who has to say sorry. And not just to me but to all the Papuan people. They have to return our sovereignty'.

And even though it is risky for us there are many times we have come out on to the streets in our thousands, even in our tens of thousands, to demand freedom.

These are just some of our stories of resistance. There are stories of resistance all over Papua.

We want you to know that building unity is not easy – but we are doing it

The Indonesian government and corporations use many methods to divide us; to turn Papuans against Papuans. If some people raise their voice, the company will come – or the government will come – and say, 'Hey, come into the office, let's talk'. They then give that person money, or a scholarship, or a good job. These are some of the ways our opponent uses to break our resistance.

But we keep taking steps to come together. There is a long history to this. When the Amungme have a problem we build a traditional house. In this house – this Tongoi – people come, sit down and talk. We invite every leader and chief from every village. People come together in one mind. When people then go out of the Tongoi they are going to bring a change. These are traditional ways of calling up assistance. In our culture, no-one can stand up by themselves. Everyone needs everyone.

So we keep taking steps to come together. We have now formed the United Liberation Movement for West Papua. Inside this united movement are the National Federal Republic of West Papua, the West Papua National Coalition of Liberation, National Committee for West Papua (KNPB), National Parliament for West Papua and other non-affiliated groups. We are strengthening our struggle, and as we do so more and more people join us. People in other Pacific nations are raising their voices.

Our resistance is like a mat or noken, many strands woven together to become one. Our resistance is like a spear, sharp and dangerous. Our resistance is like a drum that speaks with the voices of the ancestors.

We want you to know about Papuan skills in survival

Despite all the injustices we have faced, we are survivors and we have many skills. We are wise about when to speak, when to stay quiet, and when to sing our songs. Some of these songs were written in prison for the future of West Papua. Some of our singers have been arrested and murdered. But we continue to sing freedom.

We also have our dances. We wear our traditional dress, and dance traditional Papuan dances. Our Papuan culture helps us to love and care for one another. When we live inside our culture we are free.

We have prayer, faith in Jesus Christ, and God as our witness.

And we have each other. We are among friends and we want to acknowledge all those who have stood with us.

There are other Papuan survival skills too.

Like mothers' skills of endurance. Mothers who sell fruit and vegetables to feed their families and send their children to school display their produce on hessian mats by the side of the road. Rain, hail, sun and dust they sit. They survive.

Some of us travelled by canoe with 43 others all the way to Australia to seek another life. Years later, some of us sailed back to West Papua with the Freedom Flotilla. The West Papuans, Aboriginal Elders and other Australian supporters on board the flotilla carried a message of peace and solidarity, and reignited ancient connections.

And we have skills in humour, in jokes and in laughter. Even in the hardest times, we pray, we sing, we dance, and somehow we find a way to laugh.

We want you to know about our hopes and our dreams

We carry a big hope together … a free West Papua. We have held onto this hope for many, many years.

As we lift up these injustices to the light, then all the other cases will also be lifted up.

And we carry a hope for justice – international justice, Western justice, West Papuan justice, spiritual justice.

That is why we are testifying today.

We are sharing with you testimonies of injustice.

We are speaking about the effects of these injustices.

We are sharing testimonies of remembrance.

We are sharing stories of resistance, action and rescue.

We are sharing our Papuan survival skills.

And we are testifying to our hopes and to our dreams.

What we are testifying to here has been an open secret. We have always known this, God has always known this, but now you will know it too.

This means that now you are also witnesses.

So these stories and our hopes will now also be carried by you.

Thank you.

At the citizens tribunal, Ronny Kareni delivered a powerful early version of this testimony. It is possible to view this online.[6] The current version included here is now being used to foster solidarity between different groups and has been performed in theatres by Aboriginal dance troupe Biddigal Performing Arts to raise consciousness about West Papuan experience, action and aspirations.

Free spaces, communities of memory and social movement

Inspired by the West Papuan independence movement, I am interested in how such collective testimonies can contribute to social movements. In this next section I explore how collective testimonies can be linked to what various thinkers have described as 'free spaces' (Allen, 1970; Couto, 1993; Polletta, 1999; Scott, 1990).

In his article, 'Narrative, free space, and political leadership in social movements', Richard A. Couto (1993) provokes us to consider the question, 'How is voice preserved so that it may emerge at times of overt insurgency or political protest?' (1993, p. 60). In seeking to answer this question he draws upon the work of political scientist, anthropologist and anarchist, James C. Scott (1990):

> Scott describes domination and resistance as matters of degree. When resistance is manifest, as in a social movement, hidden transcripts become public. When domination prevails, voice is expressed further and further from public view and within safe and free spaces of the oppressed. At the height of repression, these spaces may be restricted to the memory of an individual or perhaps the family (Scott, 1990, pp. 3, 65, 92, 148). Scott thus suggests that free spaces preserve voice even at times when there are no social movements that overtly resist domination ... what is the content of the 'hidden transcripts'; how do they support resistance; and how are oppressed people transformed by them. (Couto, 1993, p. 60)

Scott's concept of free spaces is an intriguing one. Can narrative practice be used to consolidate, enlarge or create such free spaces? Couto believes the 'creation of free spaces, beyond the family, wherein narratives extol the virtues of community members' to be a key political task (Couto, 1993, p. 63).

I believe the West Papuan collective testimony creates such a free space in which the aspirations of West Papuan independence are embedded in rich histories of resistance. It is, at the same time, a call to action. As

Frederick W. Mayer (2014) describes:

> Those who would move collective action seek to ... pull their
> audience onto the stage, transforming each person from an
> interested bystander to an actor in the social drama, an actor
> in history. And they try to foster the apprehension that this
> moment in the social drama is also the crucible of each person's
> autobiographical narrative, a self-defining moment when they will
> be forced to answer the question: 'What did you do when history
> called?' (Mayer, 2014, p. 127)

The final words of the testimony reverberate among witnesses long
after they are first heard:

> What we are testifying here has been an open secret. We have
> always known this, God has always known this, but now you will
> know it too.
> This means that now you are also witnesses.
> So these stories and our hopes will now also be carried by you.
> Thank you.

Healing and justice together[7]

As well as preserving voice, creating free space and making a call to action,
this collective testimony, and the tribunal in which it was delivered, can
also be seen as bringing together the often polarised concepts of healing
and justice.

There are many different conceptualisations of justice. Here in Australia,
prior to invasion and colonisation, there were 350 to 700 different language
groups. There were multiple and diverse legal systems and concepts of
justice. While the effects of colonisation continue to be devastating across
this land, multiple Indigenous languages and systems of law/lore remain.
But they are rarely recognised by the wider community.

My great-great-grandfather Sir Samuel Griffith was a lawyer who came to Australia from Wales and became the first Chief Justice of Australia. He was also centrally involved in drafting the Australian Constitution, which not only imposed one system of European English law over 350 to 750 existing Indigenous legal systems, but also failed to acknowledge that these 350 to 700 legal systems even existed. When our ancestors have done things that we profoundly regret, I think we have a duty to our ancestors, as well as a duty to others, to try to understand what this means and to work in partnerships to explore different ways forward (Denborough, 2014).

I think these histories, and our present, pose weighty challenges to us here in Australia, particularly because our so-called justice system is one of the major sources of injustice in our land; not only of historical injustice, but continuing injustice. What does it mean for us if we are the receivers of stories of injustice, and our so-called justice system is actually a system of injustice?

Injustice system

To my mind, there are three profound ways in which our so-called justice system perpetuates injustice. The first is one that I've already alluded to: our legal system – the police, the courts and the prison system – has been, and continues to be, one of the primary forces of colonisation in this country. This is painfully illustrated by the vast over-representation of Aboriginal and Torres Strait Islander people in prison and the effects this has on communities throughout the country.

The second way in which our 'justice system' perpetuates injustice relates to the vast majority of people in our country who experience violence – child sexual abuse survivors, survivors of sexual assault and those who experience domestic violence. Taken together, these three groups represent a majority of people who experience violence in our country. And yet our justice system does not create justice for the vast majority of those children, women and men. In fact, for many survivors of sexual violence, child abuse and domestic violence, the criminal justice system doesn't offer healing or justice, and in fact regularly contributes to retraumatisation. If the majority of people who experience violence and personal injustice in our country don't find justice or healing in our justice system, this poses a profound challenge.

And then there is a third realm. We often think that the prison system is an appropriate response to violence. This is our accepted cultural or societal response to violence. But this involves ignoring that prisons are themselves institutions of violence and degradation. Violence occurs regularly in every prison, in all our major cities. This violence is particularly directed at the most vulnerable inmates, such as those who are young, gay or transgender, but the degradation and violence of prisons is institutional (Denborough & Preventing Prisoner Rape Project, 2005). It is really only possible to uphold prisons as our societal response to violence if we choose to ignore the violence that happens in our prisons every day.

For those of us interested in justice, these are three profound challenges. If, as counsellors and community workers, we are the receivers of stories of social suffering, if we are the receivers of stories of violence, if we are the receivers of stories of injustice, then what are our responsibilities? How are we to respond? Once we acknowledge that we have a profound and often unnamed and unacknowledged problem in our country – that our 'justice system' in many ways perpetuates injustice – then what are we to do? Perhaps we can't leave matters of justice only to lawyers and the legal system. Perhaps we can question how our work can contribute to both healing and justice.

What is this going to look like? I'm not really sure, but one starting point might involve beginning to notice, sometimes resurrect and sometimes co-create, a great diversity of forms of justice – processes in which justice and healing are not separated. This is something that I think we, as counsellors and community workers, can participate in.

If we are to find or create supplementary forms of justice/healing, then I suspect these will be generated through cross-cultural partnerships and involve explorations of diverse cultural meanings. Indeed, the West Papuan collective testimony and the way in which it continues to be enacted seems to offer us signposts. The West Papuans in their collective testimony name four different forms of justice: 'international justice, Western justice, West

Papuan justice, spiritual justice'. What's more, I believe the development of this testimony and its performance at the citizens tribunal and in other contexts is in itself an example of a further kind of 'narrative justice', one that is not separate from healing.

To my mind, this form of 'narrative justice' includes:

- naming and acknowledging multiple injustices and multiple effects

- remembrance and evoking a 'community of memory'

- eliciting, naming and acknowledging what has survived – survival skills, shared ideals, values, hopes and dreams

- convening forums of narrative justice.

Let me explain what I mean by each of these.

Naming and acknowledging multiple injustices and multiple effects

Over years we have faced one injustice after another and then another . . .

First, the testimony names and acknowledges the multiple injustices that people have experienced. The process elicited in fine detail, in people's own words, different injustices that have been (and are being) endured, and then found ways that these could be richly witnessed and acknowledged in resonant ways. What's more, the multiple effects of these injustices are also named and acknowledged in ways that fit with local culture.

Remembrance and evoking a 'community of memory'

We have always remembered those who were killed. We will remember them until we die.

If they knew that we were meeting together now, if they knew that we were gathering this testimony, they would be very happy. This would mean something to them.

Memory does not only reside in the minds of individuals. Memory can be conceived of as both interior and exterior.[8] Exterior memory resides, or is performed, in memorial sites, in rituals, in conversations, in photographs, in documents, in relationships and also in performances of collective testimonies. It is possible to understand memory as not only something that is experienced by an individual, but also as something that people do together.

This West Papuan collective testimony evokes a particular form of memory. Influenced by narrative concepts of listening for multiple storylines, it generates multi-storied remembrance (see Denborough, 2010b). It honours both loss and legacy. In this collective testimony, the 're-membering' concept within narrative therapy (M. White, 1988, 2007) has found a collective narrative form. The process did not require people to speak in an individual voice for themselves. It did not require intense, private, individual engagements with history. Instead, the process involved the creation and performance of social memory through collective testimony.

Significantly, in this testimony, the values, survival skills and knowledges that were demonstrated by lost loved ones prior to the Biak Massacre, and prior to the occupation, become linked to initiatives taken by those in the present. This testimony acknowledges how legacies from those who have died are now being carried through the present and into the future.

Whenever this testimony is 'performed', it involves a ritual that creates a 'usable past', a past that can be the basis for action in the present and future.[9] This emphasis on linking remembrance to action seems significant, as Richard Couto explains:

Bellah et. al (1985) suggest that the communities of memory nurture individuals by carrying on moral traditions that reinforce the aspirations of their group (p. 286). The test of this community is its sense of common past. The telling and retelling of stories establishes that past and offers 'examples of the men and women who have embodied and exemplified the meaning of the community.' In addition, there are stories of suffering 'that sometimes creates deeper identities than success.' These stories approximate a moral tradition and turn community of memory members 'toward the future as communities of hope' (p. 153). Such communities of hope sponsor transforming social movements. (Cuoto, 1993, p. 60)

Could it be that multi-storied testimonies, like the one by the West Papuans, could contribute in some small way to the sustenance of communities of memory and hope, which might, in turn, sponsor continuing action and social movement? If so, is this contributing to a particular form of 'narrative justice', one that brings a different relationship to both grief and action?

Eliciting, naming and acknowledging what has survived – survival skills, shared ideals, values, hopes and dreams

We carry a big hope together … a free West Papua. We have held onto this hope for many, many years.

The testimony is very clear about what has been destroyed by the injustices of the occupation of West Papua and how the effects of this are continuing. At the same time, however, it is also very clear about what has survived. By this, the testimony points out that despite injustices and violence, survivors remain connected to, and committed to, certain ideals and values in life. Whomever we are working with, we can listen for the values, the self-transcending ideals, that are implicit within survivors' expressions of anguish (see Benson, 2001; M. White, 2000). We can make it possible for survivors to name these shared ideals and explore their social histories. We can notice and acknowledge the ways in which survivors have already enacted these ideals. And we create contexts in which survivors can contribute to the further perpetuation of these shared ideals (see Denborough, 2010b). This process involves 'doing justice' to stories of survival.

Sharon Welch (1990) has described a number of elements that she believes are 'essential to maintain resistance in the face of overwhelming odds' (1990, p. 20). These include a 'redefinition of responsible action' and a 'grounding in community':

Responsible action does not mean one individual resolving the problems of others. It is, rather, participation in a communal work, laying the groundwork for the creative response of people in the present and in the future. Responsible action means changing what can be altered in the present even though a problem is not completely resolved. Responsible action provides partial resolutions and the inspiration and conditions for further partial resolution by others. It is sustained and enabled by participation in a community of resistance. (Welch, 1990, p. 75)

To my mind, the West Papuan testimony provides a 'community of resistance' based on such notions of responsible action.

By tracing the histories of what has survived, the testimony and its performance also contribute to the sustenance of a 'heritage of resistance' (Welch, 1990, p. 75), a heritage that is conveyed and transmitted in each retelling. Sharon Welch describes that within contexts of potentially overwhelming odds, one of the basic requirements for community members to contribute to 'further work for justice' is 'the creation and maintenance of self-respect in the face of people and institutions who violate an individual's, a people's sense of self worth' (Welch, 1990, p. 76). The West Papuan collective testimony and the ceremonies within which it is performed provide powerful definitions of self and collective-respect.

Convening forums of narrative justice

Within the citizens tribunal, which was mostly run in the style of a coronial inquiry, the collective testimony had a particular part to play, as Jason MacLeod described:

It reclaimed the space of the courtroom, placing Papuan culture and Papuan aspirations centre stage. This fundamentally changed the energy of the Tribunal. (MacLeod, personal communication, 2016)[10]

The engagement of narrative practices also enabled the tribunal to be an experience of healing as well as justice-seeking. When testimonies offered in tribunals or courts are double-storied (see Denborough, 2005), there is a chance for both justice and witnesses to be protected.

The tribunal became a unique forum, one of activism, healing and a search for justice. As the testimony continues to be told and performed at conferences and in theatres, it's also possible to conceive of these forums and ceremonies as rituals of alternative justice or narrative justice. In these public events, survivors' testimonies continue to honour loss and legacy, to remember the dead and to treasure the dream and determination of a free West Papua.

Narrative practice, social movement, community organising and strategy

The collective testimony described in this chapter is just one example of how collective narrative practices are being put to work to support social movements. Couto (1993) believes that the 'theoretical significance of narratives as a support of social movements opens up a field for political psychology' (1993, p. 62). I agree wholeheartedly. There is much to explore.

In addition to social movement theorists like Cuoto engaging with the narrative metaphor, in recent years, community organisers[11] have been doing similarly. Most notably, Marshall Ganz (2011), in his paper 'Public narrative, collective action, and power', has described ways in which engagement with narratives can motivate action for social change. Ganz is particularly interested in training community organisers to hone and retell a 'story of self', 'story of us' and 'story of now' to motivate people to engage in social action:[12]

Stories, strategically told, can powerfully rouse a sense of urgency, hope, anger, solidarity, and the belief that individuals, acting in concert, can make a difference. (Ganz, 2011, pp. 288–289)

This strategic use of the narrative form is aligned with a form of community organising and leadership linked to the Saul Alinksy tradition[13] (See Alinsky, 1971; Walls, 2015). Although I am less interested in the strategic use of narrative as a form of leadership practice, I'm vitally interested in how narrative practices can be engaged with and by communities to generate and sustain social change. It's early days in this regard but I will include four examples of sparkling work that perhaps offer glimpses of bringing together community organising and narrative practice.[14]

Creative interventions and the StoryTelling and Organizing Project

Creative Interventions[15] and the StoryTelling and Organizing Project (STOP)[16] are community projects based in North America which build upon the inspiring work of INCITE![17] and Critical Resistance[18] in seeking an end to both interpersonal/intimate violence and the violence of police and prison systems. Creative Interventions was developed to foster the development of community-based interventions addressing interpersonal violence. STOP, facilitated by Rachel Herzing and Issac Ontiveros, is continuing this:

Many people have been developing community-based interventions to interpersonal violence. By that we mean:

- Actions taken to stop, address or prevent interpersonal violence

- Community-based or collective action – involving family, friends, neighbours, co-workers, community members

- Actions that do not rely on social services, police or child protective services

While many of us support the idea of community-based responses to violence, some of us have difficulty even imagining what this could look like … What can we learn from stories? We can learn a lot about what works and what doesn't. We can find out what helped survivors feel supported or what helped people change to stop their violence. We can get good ideas about how family, friends, neighbors, and community members can create safety and accountability among ourselves. We can build healthy, self-determined communities. (STOP, n.d.)

This project, and its approach to community organising, is one that involves both action and imagination. It is also elicitive, in that it seeks to highlight, document and share grassroots initiatives, and in so doing, build possibilities for wider changes.

Plataforma d'Afectats per la Hipoteca-Lleida

In Spain, two narrative practitioners, Mònica Florensa and Jordi Freixas, have been working in conjunction with the social movement Plataforma d'Afectats per la Hipoteca-Lleida (Platform of people Affected by Mortgages – PAH),[19] which supports people who have lost their home or are in danger of losing their home in a foreclosure because they cannot meet their mortgage payments. PAH seeks to organise in order to resist evictions and to obtain support for people who have lost their jobs and cannot afford their mortgages.

A collective session was facilitated by Mònica and Jordi using a narrative approach, in which members could speak about their personal histories and the actions they have been taking in particular ways. These conversations generated a textual heritage[20] of achievement, as Mònica Florensa described:

As people spoke of the many goals that PAH members have achieved, we wrote down their words. These included stories of negotiations with banks; debts being forgiven; repossessions of property that had been stopped; social (protected) leases that have been obtained; success in invalidating abusive clauses within mortgage contracts; managing to get special electricity and gas contracts for people who can't afford the usual tariffs; the creation of urban gardens; the occupation of flats so that the banks have not been able to re-sell these; protests that have raised awareness, put pressure on banks; and creating a new consciousness of the whole picture in Spain. It was also particularly relevant for us to speak about how PAH is a collective of mutual help between equals – a space of solidarity, trust and belonging.

We are determined to minimize the damage that problems with mortgages have done or could do to other members of PAH. Even if members have not received any advantages for themselves personally, they spoke of the significance of finding out that they were capable of generating changes that were beneficial for somebody else. This aspect of our work together enhances personal agency and empowers each and every member.

The participants were especially proud of their capacity to support newcomers to PAH when they come to their first meeting. On that day, they arrive struggling with a powerful feeling of guilt and failure, seeing no way out and we, as a team, help them to change that feeling into hope and critical thinking.

Sharing experiences in this session allowed a socializing of skills and knowledge. Those affected by the treacherous mortgage are no longer passive subjects, nor victims that are assisted by an expert, we become, instead, active subjects who convey and share knowledge. All this together produces an amplifying effect.

A collective document was created from the words of the participants and it was read at the following meeting of the assembly of PAH. It was approved and applauded by the assembly and was then was hung on the wall to make visible the goals that have been achieved. PAH sent a translated version of this document to West Papuan and Brazilian activists, who responded with messages of solidarity. These messages were also displayed on the walls of the regular meeting room. In addition, narrative practices have been used to make a video to publicise the struggle of PAH. This video has become a collective visual document for PAH in Lleida which makes visible the ways people have been able to affect change.

Collective narrative practices have enabled members of PAH to create a different sense of teamwork, to generate a common history, and to articulate what values have sustained us. (Mònica Florensa, personal communication, 4 May 2017)

Figure 19. Plataforma d'Afectats per la Hipoteca-Lleida (Platform of people Affected by Mortgages) meeting in Barcelona
Source: Mònica Florensa.

A third example of a collective narrative practice linked to a social movement is described here by IP Kim-Ching of Hong Kong.

A collective narrative practice inspired by the Umbrella Movement in Hong Kong by IP Kim-Ching

In the autumn and winter of 2014, tens of thousands of people took to the streets of Hong Kong to demand genuine universal suffrage and a free and fair democratic system. The protests were a response to reforms to the electoral system announced by the Standing Committee of the National People's Congress. These reforms were seen as ultra-conservative and as establishing the Chief Executive of Hong Kong as a puppet of the Chinese Communist Party. To disperse the huge number of peaceful demonstrators, Hong Kong police used tear gas and batons and even threatened to open gunfire. The series of protests was referred to as the Umbrella Movement because participants used umbrellas to defend themselves against the tear gas spray. The brutal police crackdown on the peaceful demonstrators drove them away from the government headquarters. They went on to occupy major roads in the Admiralty, Causeway Bay and Mong Kok areas. These three 'Occupy' areas were held for a very long 79 days and nights, until they were finally cleared by the Hong Kong government and police.

After the crackdown

The Umbrella Movement was eventually shut down by the government. The demands of the protestors were unfulfilled. However, many participants remained committed to their dreams and quite a number of civic groups were formed to further enhance democracy and work towards genuine universal suffrage for Hong Kong's people. Many of the students and others who participated in the Umbrella Movement experienced emotional upheavals in its aftermath, including feelings of hopelessness, helplessness, depression, anger, loss of meaning and loss of direction. Because of my work as a clinical psychologist and my participation in the movement, I was often asked to talk to fellow participants who had been negatively influenced by the events and the related difficult feelings. In the tradition of collective narrative practice, I developed a localised collective exercise, the Umbrella of Life, with another narrative practitioner. This was used with groups of people who had participated in the Umbrella Movement. Through the exercise, in which an umbrella was used as a symbol of resistance, people could retell their stories and bear witness to each other. Through such retellings and mutual witnessing, people reconnected with one another through their shared values, beliefs, hopes and dreams.

The Umbrella of Life process

We began the group process by introducing the use of umbrellas in daily life, including as protection from rain and sun. We also reminded the group of the versatility of the umbrella, as demonstrated during the Umbrella Movement when umbrellas were our companions in resisting tear gas spray, and were joined together to consolidate lines of defence. We discussed the umbrella as a symbol of our resistance and a source of protection for our hopes and dreams. When they were ready, the participants were asked to draw an umbrella with:

- a handle, where participants could write down what influenced them and gave them energy, be it family, religion, a person, a place, a song or anything in life

- a shaft, where participants could write down their skills, knowledge and strengths

- ribs, where participants could write down their hopes and dreams (including for future social change)

- a canopy, where participants could write down what is important to them and what they want to defend.

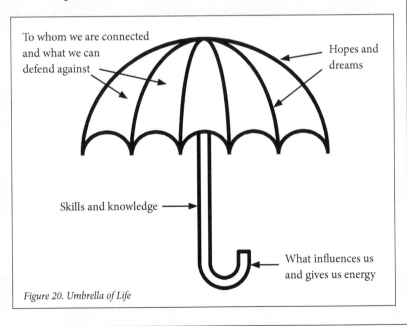

To whom we are connected and what we can defend against

Hopes and dreams

Skills and knowledge

What influences us and gives us energy

Figure 20. Umbrella of Life

Each participant was then interviewed about their personal umbrella stories so that the descriptions on the different parts of the umbrella picture could be further drawn out and built upon.

When all the umbrellas were brought together, group discussion focused on the following areas of enquiry:

- What are the externalised problems we are currently up against? These included reactions of hopelessness and other emotions that people were experiencing after the crackdown on the Umbrella Movement.

- What dreams can be achieved and what is it possible for us to defend ourselves against?

An umbrella story

To illustrate the process of the Umbrella of Life, I will share Chloe's story (Chloe is a pseudonym). On the handle of her umbrella, Chloe wrote down 'seeking truth' and 'the need to take action for what you believe'. On the shaft, she wrote 'be persistent in your belief', 'breakthrough for oneself' and 'influence other people'. Her hope was to get 'justice for Hong Kong people', and she wanted to defend 'everyone having their human rights and freedom, and the right not to be harmed and exploited'.

Chloe's personal stories were further elicited. When asked about who had influenced her desire to seek truth, Chloe described a secondary school science teacher who emphasised the use of detailed analysis and trial and error to find out the truth about the physical world. She thought the same spirit and method could help her to search for social justice too. When asked about her commitment to 'everyone having their human rights and freedom', Chloe told of her experience joining Amnesty International in Hong Kong as a high school student. After volunteering with Amnesty, Chloe wanted to learn more about violations of human rights in different countries, and about prisoners of conscience and political prisoners. She developed a determination to protect human rights around the world. After re-membering and reconnecting with her personal stories through the Umbrella of Life process, Chloe felt reinvigorated and more strongly connected to her commitments and agency. She also felt more able to resist the hopelessness and other negative emotions she had experienced in the aftermath of the crackdown on the Umbrella Movement.

Reflections

Although the Umbrella Movement was shut down and there are still no signs that genuine universal suffrage will be achieved in Hong Kong, we still have our 'right to define our experience and problems in our own words and terms' (Denborough, 2015). With these storytelling rights, we maintain our hope and continue to strive for justice, freedom and democracy.

Heritage of achievement and strategy

To bring this chapter to a close, I wish to return to a further example from the work of West Papuan activists and Jason MacLeod. It involves an adaption of the Team of Life narrative approach[21] (Denborough, 2008) in order to discuss strategy. Football is keenly followed in West Papua, and this approach uses sporting metaphors to celebrate previous successful strategies in order to then consider future actions. After creating a 'teamsheet' that acknowledges the key members, supporters and coach of the 'team' that is seeking change, it is then possible to use sporting metaphors to generate a heritage of achievement and explore realms of strategy.

The following edited extract is from MacLeod and Whelan (2015, pp. 121–126).

Creating a strategy board by Jason MacLeod

The first step involves naming a goal that your team (campaign) has already achieved. Draw a football field and illustrate how this goal was achieved as if it were a goal in football. Include everyone who was involved and describe the parts they played. Also mark on the strategy board the key strategies and tactics that were used.

The strategy board below illustrates how Tongoi Papua, an independent union of West Papuan mine workers at the giant Freeport/Rio Tinto Copper and Gold mine, won a 100% wage increase.

Tongoi Papua's campaign began with reconciling competing factions (proses rekonsiliasi). After that they held a gathering (mubes) where the problems West Papuan mine workers faced could be discussed and analysed and strategies and tactics debated. The next step was preparing to strike (persiapan mogok) followed by a 28-day campaign (Kampanye 28 hari) in which a diverse range of tactics was employed. When Freeport still did not concede to Tongoi Papua's demands, 9 000 mine workers walked off the job.

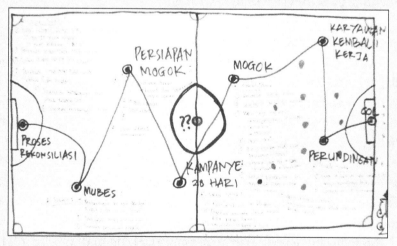

Figure 21. A Tongoi Papua strategy board
Source: Jason MacLeod

When the company agreed to negotiations (perundingan) they went back to work (kembali kerja). Finally (gol) they achieved a nearly 100% wage increase for the lowest paid worker.

Re-enactment

This is the fun part! Each team re-enacts the goal as a drama, as if they were at the main stadium on grand final day. Ask someone to be the commentator whose job is to retell the goal and all the steps that took place. Perhaps the drama will sound something like, 'Here we are at xx stadium and it's the [name of campaign team] versus the [name of the opponent]. It's been a tough season but the [name of campaign team] have been in training for a long time and here they go, they're off!' The commentator then describes all the steps.

Before you start, ask people how they celebrate when their team scores a goal and they are in the crowd. Generate a big list of all the different ways participants in the group celebrate. Then when one campaign is retelling their goal with all the strategies they have used, the rest of the group are the supportive spectators, so by the time the commentator actually says GOALLLLLL, all the spectators start cheering and jumping up and down and going wild. Depending what the group is like, this can be done with a real football with different people re-enacting the parts of the campaign, or for the more reserved or serious it's possible to simply have the commentator and crowd getting wild in response to a retelling rather than a re-performance!

After this re-enactment there's a chance to go over the successful strategies and key learnings from the example. These learnings can be documented and shared.

Planning future strategy

A similar process can then be used to draw up and discuss detailed strategies for present and future campaigns. In doing so, it can be significant to map out and analyse the 'opposition team' (as if they were a football team):

- Who plays for the opponent? (include things like poverty, despair, fear etc. – whatever the practical obstacles are to our campaigns)

- What positions does the opponent have?

- Who plays what position?

- What are their special moves?

- Who is sitting on the bench?

- Who is the opponent's coach?

- Do they have a sponsor?

- Is there a team song or cheer squad that is used to boast morale?

- Why do the players play for this team?

- How committed are the opponent's team members? Why are they committed? What might change that commitment? What are their motivations and interests? What would it take for some of the opponent's players join your team?

This adaption of the Team of Life approach by Jason MacLeod is the first example that I know of that uses narrative practices to assist in community organising strategy.

Narrative practice and social movement

This chapter has explored how collective testimonies and other narrative methodologies are being used to support social movements and community organising. At the same time, it has described early attempts to bring together considerations of healing and justice. As social movement theorists and community organisers continue to engage with the narrative metaphor, I am looking forward to further explorations.

Notes

1. See www.biak-tribunal.org/background/
2. See the ABC News 7:30 special broadcast: Searching for the truth about a massacre in West Papua: www.abc.net.au/7.30/content/2013/s3912701.htm
3. See www.biak-tribunal.org/introduction-and-musical-welcome/
4. It was an invitation from Jason MacLeod to Dulwich Centre Foundation that led to our involvement in the Biak Massacre Citizens Tribunal. Jason's interest in how collective narrative practices might contribute to community organising has also been significant in the development of this chapter. To read more about Jason's work, see MacLeod (2015).
5. The first part of the first page of the testimony is drawn from Theo van den Broek and Budi Hernawan's work on Memoria Passionis (memory of suffering) in West Papua (Hernawan & Broek, 1999).
6. See www.biak-tribunal.org/a-collective-testimony/
7. The Just Therapy Team – Charles Waldegrave, Taimalie Kiwi Tamasese, Flora Tuhaka and Warihi Campbell (2003) – have for many years invited and challenged the field of family therapy not to separate healing and justice. For more discussion of forms of narrative practice that bring together healing and justice see Hung and Denborough (2013) and Denborough (2013).
8. For more about the exteriorisation of memory, see Jedlowski (2001).
9. For more on the concept of a 'usable past', see Denborough, Wingard and C. White (2009).
10. See www.biak-tribunal.org/a-collective-testimony/
11. For an excellent introduction to the field of community organising see Walls (2015).
12. See marshallganz.usmblogs.com/files/2012/08/Public-Narrative-Worksheet-Fall-2013-.pdf
13. Michael White, in his paper 'Narrative practice and community assignments' (2003), clarifies the relationship between community organising and narrative practice:

    There is a tradition of community organising and advocacy that is highly valued and has been effective in assisting communities to address a range of social phenomena, particularly those that contribute to structures of disadvantage and racism ... At times, our work with communities has been taken by others to be of this tradition of community organising and advocacy. Although this is a tradition that we value highly, we are not community organisers or advocates in the context of our community assignments. Our work is of a different tradition, and engages us in different practices with communities. (M. White, 2003, p. 24)

14. Jason MacLeod, in response to an earlier draft of this chapter, noted that in his experience narrative is used in every part of the community organising cycle:

Narrative is used as a way of bonding and building relationships, not just between organisers and potential leaders but also between people in organisations and groups and also across organisational, race, class, ethnic and religious lines. In many community organising traditions, people get trained to explore one another's biographies, particularly those stories that speak to why people do what they do – or why they don't – as well as the stories that shape people's preferred identities. Narrative is also used in listening campaigns, and as part of a discernment process in determining what issues people have appetite to organise around, and the framing of those issues. Once people decide what to work on, strategies and tactics get disseminated through double-storied testimonies, ones that illustrate the problem, its effects on people and why people are determined to do something about it. As the campaign gets going, story is used again to highlight particular norms like courage and determination. At the end of the campaign, stories become a way of evaluating. Success is not only about achieving the campaign's stated goals. Organisers also search out stories that speak to how people built power; how campaigning might have shifted the political weather; the way people talked about or understood the issue. Organisers also use stories as ways to build organisations and foster alliances between groups.

15. See www.creative-interventions.org/

16. See www.stopviolenceeveryday.org/stop-2/

17. See www.incite-national.org/

18. See criticalresistance.org/

19. See www.facebook.com/PAHLleida/

20. The term 'textual heritage' was proposed by Lowenthal (1994) as quoted in Wertsch (2002, p. 62).

21. See dulwichcentre.com.au/team-of-life/

PART IV

A STORYLINE OF
COLLECTIVE NARRATIVE PRACTICE

Chapter 9

A history of ideas, social projects and partnerships

Collective narrative practice is an emerging field. Building on the thinking and practice foundations of narrative therapy (Epston, 1989a; M. White, 1989; M. White & Epston, 1989, 1990), collective narrative practice seeks to respond to groups and communities that have experienced significant social suffering in contexts in which 'therapy' may not be culturally resonant. This chapter tells the story of my path through this emerging field. It provides an intellectual history of six key aspects of narrative therapy and richly describes a range of social projects and partnerships. I hope this historical tale will contribute to the literature about the social and intellectual origins of narrative therapy.[1] I also hope this chapter will provide a historical foundation for the field of collective narrative practice.

In writing this paper, I have returned to texts that Michael White and David Epston wrote in the 1980s, prior to the naming of 'narrative therapy', and to the sources they were drawing on. Alongside this intellectual history, collective narrative practice has also emerged from experiences, relationships, encounters and cross-cultural and cross-gender partnerships. This chapter describes my journey through all of this. It is a journey that began in 1993.

In 1993, at 23 years of age, I was living in Sydney. A few years earlier, I had graduated from social work, and I was working in a maximum security prison within the welfare and education units. This involved facilitating groups for transgender inmates and for young men who had recently been imprisoned, and 'teaching' about issues of class, gender and race within a welfare course for inmates who hoped to work in this area when they were released. At the same time, I was volunteering to meet regularly with young men in schools about considerations of gender and violence.

Looking back at this time in my life, I can see that I was really struggling to work out how to respond to what were, for me, two relatively recent discoveries: colonisation and the effects of dominant masculinities.

My family tree had been 'replanted in someone else's yard'[2]

Working within prisons meant that I was now in contact and forming significant connections with representatives of the First Nations of Australia. Before working in prisons, I had never to my knowledge met Aboriginal people. I had certainly never before tried to understand my life through the lens of Indigenous Australia. I had never before grappled with how police and prisons in Australia represent the continuing occupation of Aboriginal lands and the continuing disenfranchisement of the poor.

The harm that people of my gender (men) had done and were continuing to do to women, to children and to other men.

Working within schools, I was meeting with young men on the cusp of adult masculinity. At times, delight, mirth and openness could be seen in their eyes. At other times, brutality and cruelty predominated. Each workshop we[3] would run in schools with MASA (Men Against Sexual Assault) involved witnessing how dominant forms of masculinity were shaping these young men's lives and trying our best to open space for other ways of being. Monday through to Wednesday I would meet with men in prison, some of whom had raped, assaulted or murdered others. And on Thursday and Friday, I would meet with young men in schools, some of whom were already convinced that they would spend part of their lives behind bars and razor wire.

At the time, I was reading everything and anything that could provide possibilities for action. This included feminist writings of the second wave (Greer, 1970; R. Morgan, 1970), poststructuralist gender theorists (Davies, 1993), and those writing about masculinities (Connell, 1987; Kimmel, 1987; Messerschmidt, 1993; Segal, 1990).

And so it was that one day I was sitting at my desk at Long Bay maximum security prison when a colleague handed me a copy of the *Dulwich Centre Newsletter* entitled 'Some thoughts on men's ways of being' (Dulwich Centre, 1992). 'I think you might be interested in this', she said.

She was right.

Some thoughts on men's ways of being

There was much about this publication that was fascinating to me, particularly a paper by Michael White entitled 'Men's culture, the men's movement, and the constitution of men's lives' (1992). Within it, Michael articulated some of the 'real effects of the essentialist project' of masculine identity (1992, p. 37) which:

- 'identifies certain "truths" about men's nature' (1992, p. 37)

- 'is inherently conservative and provocative of a paralysing form of nostalgia for what never was' (1992, p. 37)

- 'recruits us into a mytho-myopic account of men's nature' (1992, p. 37)

- 'blinds us to our complicity in the maintenance of the domination and abuse of others, and to our support of economic, political and social structures that preserve and further men's privilege' (1992, p. 38)

- 'incites men to separate from and to distance from women' (1992, p. 39).

He then proposed an 'alternative perspective on the personal, a perspective that brings the personal and the political together' (M. White, 1992, p. 35). He referred to this as a 'constitutionalist perspective' which proposed that:

- 'an objective knowledge of the world is not possible; that knowledges are actually generated in particular discursive fields in specific cultures at specific times' (1992, p. 40)

- 'all essentialist notions about human nature are actually ruses that disguise what is really taking place' (1992, p. 40)

- 'the descriptions that we have of life are not representations or reflections of life as lived, but are directly constitutive of life' (1992, p. 40)

- 'identity is multi-sited, and that it is a product of the ongoing negotiation of multiple subjectivities' (1992, p. 43).

Within this paper, Michael drew on writings of Foucault (1979, 1984, 1988; Gordon 1980), Billig and colleagues (1988), Sawicki (1991), Edward Bruner (1986) and Jerome Bruner (1990), and provided what was for me an entirely new way to understand identity. This provided new possibilities for action:

The constitutionalist perspective proposes more than just a challenge to the essentialist project and to its negative real effects. And it is provocative of more than a determination to separate our lives from the problematic aspects of the dominant men's culture. It also provokes a determination to engage in processes that generate and/or resurrect alternative knowledges and practices of men's ways of being, and that lead to the development and the performance of alternative narratives of self that have preferred real effects. (M. White, 1992, p. 43)

It was this article by Michael White that introduced me to a narrative perspective – one that draws together the personal and the political in particular ways:

I have proposed an alternative frame of reference for men's attempts to transform the dominant men's culture, one that I have referred to as the constitutionalist perspective. I believe that this perspective makes it possible for us to face and to come to terms with our history, and frees us to do something that is very difficult – that is, to take the courage and to find the wherewithal to act against our own culture. It is a perspective that draws together the personal and the political at several levels. (M. White, 1992, p. 51)

I was gripped. Could these ideas provide new options for the conversations I was having in prisons and schools? And what could they possibly mean for how I understood my own life and relationships?

There was something else that was profoundly significant to me about 'Some thoughts on men's ways of being' (Dulwich Centre, 1992). The papers and interviews were by both men and women and the note from the editorial team (Cheryl White, Maggie Carey and Chris McLean) indicated that this publication was the result of gender partnerships. What were these gender partnerships? What could they make possible? How did they come about?

Later, I learnt that these gender partnerships and the development of the publication 'Some thoughts on men's ways of being' were due to a challenge from Taimalieutu Kiwi Tamasese and the Just Therapy Team from New Zealand, as Cheryl White describes:

[Taimalieutu Kiwi Tamasese] said something to me that made a huge difference to my approach to these issues [of culture and gender]. She said that she knew that I was genuinely concerned about women from other cultures, but that to her, I was more like a white man than I was like a woman of colour. This wasn't personal. She said that she believed that, in terms of lived experience and privilege, white feminists are more like white men than we are like women of colour. And therefore, she said it was our responsibility to work with white men. 'Go and work with the people who you can influence', she said! And so I did. I went and worked with white men on issues of gender in all kinds of ways ... For some years, Dulwich Centre Publications focused its energy on issues of men and masculinity. With other women, we held workshops, took up petitions, tried to encourage the development of ways of working with men around issues of violence, and published a number of journal issues which ended up as a book. I have often joked that a lot of men in Australia wished I hadn't listened to Kiwi! As I saw it, an apprenticeship was required in which I and other white feminist women needed to work within our own culture on issues of gender before seeking to work in partnership across cultures. We also needed to develop a network of people connected to Dulwich

Centre Publications who were willing and wanting to address issues of gender and culture, and this gradually developed. (Yuen & C. White, 2007, pp. 23–24)

It was this social history of partnerships that had led to the publication of 'Some thoughts on men's ways of being'. On page 69 of that publication, I read the following advertisement:

Family therapy training – 1993
One week intensives with Michael White

This course will provide an introduction to a 're-authoring therapy'. This therapy is premised on an idea that the lives and relationships of persons are shaped by the very knowledges and stories that people use to give meaning to their experiences, and by certain practices of self and of relationship that are associated with these knowledges and stories. A re-authoring therapy contributes to persons resolving problems by, (a) enabling them to separate their lives and relationships from knowledges/stories that are impoverishing, (b) assisting them to challenge practices of self and of relationship that are subjugating, and (c) by encouraging persons to re-author their lives according to alternative and preferred knowledges/ stories and practices of self and of relationship that have preferred outcomes.

Intrigued by the prospect of 'reauthoring lives', I registered a place.

John McLeod has proposed that narrative therapy represents a 'postpsychological perspective' (McLeod, 2004, 2007) and that it can be described as 'cultural work' (McLeod, 2005). What brought me to Adelaide was a search for ways to respond to issues of culture, including masculinity, violence and other forms of injustice.

The ideas and practices of narrative therapy

During the intensive I stayed in a youth hostel just around the corner from Dulwich Centre. A number of my roommates were accomplished snorers, so, as sleep was not really an option, each night I took the opportunity to go over the notes I had taken during the day. There was so much happening that week. Two related realms were equally influential: the ideas and practices of the 'reauthoring therapy' as taught by Michael White, and the social projects with which Dulwich Centre was engaged.

Each night in the living room of the youth hostel, I found myself revisiting a number of themes that I believe are directly relevant to the development of collective narrative practices:

- placing personal problems back into the realm of culture and history: externalising

- the narrative metaphor and narrative practice

- counter documents and therapeutic letters

- the significance of partnerships

- an anthropology of problems and archiving alternative knowledges

- folk psychology and performed identity.

I will now describe these themes in ways that I could not have done in 1993. And as I do so, I will also briefly trace the intellectual history of these ideas that I found so exciting in 1993 and still do.

Placing personal problems back into the realm of culture and history: Externalising

Rather than locating problems within individuals, narrative practices locate personal problems in the realms of culture and history. As McLeod explains, this involves '"moving out" into the stories of a culture rather than "moving in" to individual personal experience' (McLeod, 1997,

p. 27). This ranges from putting the problem of encopresis back into children's culture as 'the "treacherous" character of the sneaky poo' (M. White, 1984, p. 153) to locating the problem of the 'voices and visions' of so-called schizophrenia outside the person and back into the realms of politics and justice:

It has been important for us to experience our work to reclaim our lives from the troublesome voices and visions as a struggle against injustice. These voices and visions are oppressive, and since our work on revising our relationship with these voices and visions addresses issues of power and control, then this relationship is a political relationship. This political understanding provides us with strength, as it keeps us in touch with the fact that we are not just on a personal journey, but also on a political journey. (Brigitte, Sue, Mem, & Veronika, 1997, p. 29)

This process of placing problems back into the realm of culture and history is now widely known as 'externalising the problem', a concept and practice that came to international prominence with the publication of *Narrative means to therapeutic ends* (White & Epston, 1990). The process was first described by Michael White in his groundbreaking papers 'Pseudo-encopresis: From avalanche to victory, from vicious to virtuous cycles' (1984) and 'Fear busting and monster taming: An approach to the fears of young children' (1985). At this stage, the word externalising was not used, but children and parents were being invited to stand together in response to 'sneaky poo' and to tame and secure 'the fears' in elaborate ways in order to attain a 'Monster and Worm Catching and Taming Certificate' or 'Fear Busting Diploma' and to achieve membership in either the 'Monster and Worm Catchers and Tamers Guild of Australia and New Zealand' or the 'Fear Busting Association of the Southern Hemisphere' (M. White, 1985, p. 111).

In 1986, in the paper 'Family escape from trouble', this process was first named as 'externalising': 'Externalizing and objectifying the problem and placing this between persons is the first step towards an interactional

definition of the problem and an interactional solution to the problem'
(M. White, 1986, p. 59).

One year on, in the paper 'Family therapy and schizophrenia:
Addressing the "in-the-corner" lifestyle' (1987), Michael White began to
draw on the writings of Michel Foucault (1979) to explain that:

> In the process of externalizing problems, cultural practices
> of objectification are utilised against cultural practices of
> objectification. The problem itself is externalized so that the person
> is not the problem. Instead, the problem is the problem. This
> objectification of and externalization of the problem challenges
> those individualizing techniques of scientific classification and
> other more general dividing practices. (M. White, 1987, p. 52)

Here is the origin of the phrase 'the person is not the problem
… the problem is the problem', which has become an emblem for
narrative practice and its externalising ethic; its refusal to pathologise or
individualise problems.

The narrative metaphor and narrative practice

'Writing your history' by David Epston (1986) was the first paper to
describe what could be called a 'narrative therapy'.[4] It described David's
conversations with Marisa, which took place in 1985 and which led him
to 'abandon the metaphor of strategy/strategic and replace it with story/
narrative' (Epston, 1989b, p. 134). Within this paper, David Epston
quoted Kenneth Gergen and Mary Gergen (1983, 1984):

> Gergen and Gergen (1983) used the term self-narratives to describe
> the social process whereby people tell stories about themselves to
> themselves and others. They characterize self-narratives as the way
> individuals … 'establish coherent connections among life events.
> Rather than seeing one's life as simply "one damned thing after

another", the individual attempts to understand life events as systematically related. They are rendered intelligible by locating them in a sequence or "unfolding process". Most events are thus not sudden and mysterious revelations, but the sensible sequence of ongoing stories.' (Epston, 1989b, p. 133)

David Epston also quoted Murray (1985) and Goffman (1959) as he brought a narrative metaphor to the field of therapy.

In Michael White's writings of the late 1980s, he made a number of references acknowledging the ways in which David Epston had been developing a unique approach to therapy based on the theory of self-narrative (M. White, 1987, p. 48) and how David had been encouraging Michael to cast his work against the text analogy (M. White, 1988b, p. 40). Encouraged also by Cheryl White's interest in the narrative metaphor through her reading of feminism (M. White, 1989, p. 12), the externalising approach of Michael White was brought together with the narrative explorations of David Epston … and suddenly so much became possible! In 1988 Michael White wrote three critical papers, each published by Dulwich Centre Publications, which had by now become a vibrant publishing house:

- 'A process of questioning: A therapy of literary merit' (1988b)

- 'Saying hullo again: The incorporation of the lost relationship in the resolution of grief' (1988a)

- 'The externalizing of the problem and the reauthoring of lives and relationships' (1988c).

And in 1989, four-and-a-half years after David Epston first met with Marisa, he met with her again. In this follow-up conversation, Marisa reflected on the experience of 'writing her history':

So the letter did a lot of good to me … to actually see it all written down. I mean you read stories and they're stories. But this wasn't a story, it was my life as I live it. And today as I think back – I couldn't have … how could I have survived all that? But I'm still here to tell the story [laughter]. (Epston, 1989b, p. 135)

In his paper 'Marisa revisits' (Epston, 1989b, p. 128), David Epston cited Barbara Hardy (1968, p. 5): 'we dream in narrative, daydream in narrative, remember, anticipate, hope, despair, believe, doubt, plan, revise, criticize, construct, gossip, learn, hate and love by narrative'.

He also quoted Lowe (1989) in order to locate these attempts to create a new form of therapy as part of a broader social project:

> we can invent a human nature that is more benign, by reinventing our categories. This must be an exercise of will and imagination. Though we can attempt to let our clients evolve their own meanings and explanations as some models suggest, that is surely impossible, we cannot not influence them … A more positive approach would be to acknowledge the degree of our influence and accept the responsibility to invent theories of people that might contribute to the formation of a more just society. (Lowe, 1989, pp. 32–33)

In 1989 David Epston and Michael White also co-authored the book *Literate means to therapeutic ends* (M. White & Epston, 1989). Influenced by the wider 'interpretive turn' occurring in anthropology and literary theory, and drawing significantly on Jerome Bruner (1986), Edward Bruner (1986), Foucault (1979, 1984, 1988), Geertz (1973, 1983), Gergen & Gergen (1984) and Goffman (1961, 1974), Michael White and David Epston proposed a therapy based on the 'reauthoring' (Myerhoff, 1982) or restorying of lives.

This reauthoring therapy is based on the premise that:

> persons experience problems, for which they frequently seek therapy, when the narratives in which they are 'storying' their experience, and/or in which they are having their experience 'storied' by others, do not sufficiently represent their lived experience, and that, in

these circumstances, there will be significant aspects of their lived experience that contradict these dominant narratives. (M. White & Epston, 1989, p. 22)

Thus the task for therapy becomes:

the identification of, or the generation of, alternative stories that enable persons to perform new meanings that bring with them desired possibilities; new meanings that persons will experience as more helpful, satisfying, and open-ended. (M. White & Epston, 1989, p. 22)

A therapy of literary merit was proposed for the elaboration and performance of these alternative stories. After *Literate means to therapeutic ends* was republished by W.W. Norton as *Narrative means to therapeutic ends*, this therapy of literary merit or reauthoring therapy gradually came to be known as 'narrative therapy'.[5]

There was, however, a further key aspect of *Literate means to therapeutic ends* that is significant to mention. This was its invitation to practitioners to consider both oral and literate traditions (Stubbs, 1980) and to investigate the therapeutic potential of practices of the written word.

Counter documents and therapeutic letters

Two-thirds of *Literate means to therapeutic ends* consisted of wide-ranging examples of therapeutic letters and counter documents that celebrated 'the new story' (M. White & Epston, 1989. p. 131). These were examples of the written word that stood in contrast with degrading psychiatric 'files':

There are those practices, situated in the domain of alternative local, popular knowledges, that have the capacity to redescribe and specify persons in ways that emphasize their special knowledges and competencies, and their place in the larger community of persons ... The practices associated with these alternative documents are in contrast with those associated with the (psychiatric) file ... Awards of various kinds, such as trophies and certificates can be considered examples of alternative documents. Such awards often signal the person's arrival at a new status in their community, one that brings with it new responsibilities and privileges. As these alternative documents have the potential of incorporating a wide readership and of recruiting an audience to the performance of new stories, they can be situated in what Myerhoff (1982) refers to as definitional ceremonies. (M. White & Epston, 1989, p. 131)

The examples of letters and documents are diverse and included:

- declarations of independence from asthma

- winning against bad habits certificates

- escaping from misery certificates

- escaping from guilt certificates.

There is now a rich tradition of documentation within narrative therapy (see also Epston, 1998, 2008; Epston & M. White, 1990; Fox, 2003; J. Freedman & Combs, 1996; Freeman, Epston, & Lobovits, 1997; Lobovits, Maisel, & Freeman, 1995; Madigan, 2011; Newman, 2008; M. White, 1995c).

The significance of partnerships

The foreword to *Literate means to therapeutic ends* was written by Karl Tomm. Within it, he wrote, 'Breaking new ground in any field is a major accomplishment. To do so in different directions at the same time, and in so doing, open up whole new territories, reflects a tour de force' (Tomm, 1989, p. 5). This tour de force represented eight years of conversation, friendship and intellectual partnership between David Epston and

Michael White. In the following extended quote, Cheryl White (2009) conveys the significance of this partnership:

[David Epston and Michael White's] enduring friendship and intellectual partnership ... was characterised by unshakable optimism, a passion over ideas, what seemed like boundless energy, and a real dedication to assist the families with whom they were meeting ... Their collaboration included stimulating challenges due to their different perspectives. Both were family therapists, but David also came from an Eriksonian background. Both were serious readers but went about this in quite different ways. David read unusually widely, calling on his background as an anthropologist, while Michael rigorously focused on one author at a time (Bateson, then Foucault and others). In fact, David was known to say that while he himself read a thousand books once, Michael read the same book a thousand times, continually finding new sources of inspiration for therapeutic practice. Appreciating each other's differences was something they shared. In the early days, if one of them was 'stuck' with a family they were seeing, they would call the other and talk it all through, generate new ideas and then go back and try them out. It seemed like almost every week there was a new development. What's more, the ideas were to be shared: '... we decided to make our ideas and practice common property and vowed that we would never become rivals. We did what we said we would do all these years up until he died ...' (Epston, 2008, p. 5).

There wasn't a sense of ownership, possession or preciousness about ideas, but instead a joy in offering them out to a world that was looking for new ways of working ... In acknowledging the contribution of both Ann Epston and Michael White to his ideas and work, David said: 'By now, I don't know where it begins and where it ends' (Epston, 1989a, p. 118).

This sentiment to me sums up the intellectual partnership between Michael White and David Epston. The origins of what is now known as narrative therapy coevolved from a shared political philosophy, and through endless hours of conversation. (C. White, 2009, pp. 50–60)

To reiterate, three distinct partnerships have already been acknowledged here that relate to the development of ideas that I engaged with in 1993 and that have gone on to shape collective narrative practices. These partnerships are:

• the partnership between David Epston and Michael White

• the partnership between the Just Therapy Team, New Zealand, (represented by Kiwi Tamalieutu Tamasese) and Dulwich Centre Publications that led to Cheryl White's determination to address and publish on issues of masculinity

• the partnership between women and men within Dulwich Centre's 'community of ideas' that led to the publication of 'Some thoughts on men's ways of being' (Dulwich Centre, 1992; McLean, Carey, & C. White, 1996).

An anthropology of problems and archiving alternative knowledges

David Epston was initially trained in anthropology and the influence of this history pervades the field of narrative practice: 'I gradually moved from undertaking anthropology as an academic pursuit, to instead finding ways in which anthropological ways of thinking could underwrite my practice as a therapist' (Epston, 2001, p. 178).

One way to describe David Epston would be as an anthropologist of problems and an archivist of alternative knowledges:

I've always thought of myself as doing research, but on problems and the relationships that people have with those problems, rather than on the people themselves. The structuring of narrative questions and interviews allow me and others to co-research problems and the alternative knowledges that are developed to address them. (Epston, 2001, p. 180)

In the 1980s, David Epston began to circulate the knowledges of those who consulted him in therapy to others who were experiencing similar difficulties. He collected client 'wisdoms', and what he referred to as client 'expert knowledge', into archives (Epston, 2001). These archives contained audiotapes, letters and artwork that represented 'a rich supply of solutions to an assortment of longstanding problems such as temper taming, night fears, school refusing, asthma, and ... anorexia and bulimia' (Madigan & Epston, 1995, p. 263). Gradually, David Epston began to create networks of clients, which he called 'leagues', so that they could provide consultation, information and support to each other. The best known example of such a league is the Anti-Anorexia/Anti-Bulimia League (Epston, 2008; Grieves, 1997; Lock, Epston, & Maisel, 2004; Lock, Epston, Maisel, & de Faria, 2005; Maisel, Epston, & Borden, 2004; Malson & Burns, 2009). Developed with David's colleague Stephen Madigan, this approach to linking groups of clients in order to share 'solution knowledges' came to be known as generating 'communities of concern' (Madigan & Epston, 1995). Employing new technologies, these communities of concern first used fax machines to send messages around the world. This was followed by online leagues to respond to various issues, including the 'Archive of resistance: Anti-anorexia/anti-bulimia'.[6]

Much of my work as a narrative therapist has been linked to my concern to act against this appropriation of knowledge in the field of the health professions. In acknowledging the alternative knowledges about life that are often co-created in re-authoring conversations, it then becomes a question of how to remain faithful to the sources of this knowledge, and how to do justice to the representation of the sources of this knowledge. This has led to the formation of leagues (for instance the Anti-Anorexia and Bulimia

League) through which the insider knowledges of those who consult therapists can be represented in ways that acknowledge the authors of this knowledge, documents the very means by which it came into being, and also makes this knowledge accessible to others.

In turn, this has led to thoughts about archives and the role of archivists. The idea of archiving has always fascinated me and in many ways I see myself as an archivist, a co-creator and anthologist of alternative knowledges. (Epston, 2001, p. 179)

This anthropological researching of problems and archiving of insider knowledges has provided a foundation for collective narrative practice.

Folk psychology and performed identity

Following Jerome Bruner (1990), David Epston and Michael White were interested in locating their narrative explorations within traditions of folk psychology. One theme that emerged through the new cultural anthropology was to consider people's realities and identities as distributed throughout communities:

With meaning at the centre, this new cultural anthropology took the focus of inquiry to the social construction of people's realities. These were realities that were not radically derived through one's independent construction of the events of one's life. These realities were not the outcome of some privileged access to the world as it is. They were not arrived at through some objective grasp of the nature of things. Rather, people's realities were understood to be historical and social products, negotiated in and between communities of people and distributed throughout these communities. This was the case for identity as much as for any other construction; identity was understood to be a phenomenon that was dispersed in communities of people, its traces to be found everywhere, including in:

- socially negotiated self-narratives,

- the impressions and the imagination of others,

- the performance of drama,

- dance, in play, in song and in poetics,

- ritual, ceremony and symbol,

- attire and in habits of life, and

- personal and public documentation, dispersed through the inscriptions entered into community stories, into personal diaries, into correspondences in the form of letters and cards, into public files in the form of profiles, assessments and reports, and in the longstanding tradition of autobiography. (White, 2001a, p. 12)

Consideration of how identity is dispersed in communities of people through drama, dance, song, ritual and documentation (see also Turner, 1986) has inspired us to explore each of these as sites for collective narrative practice.

Returning to the youth hostel

When I attended my first intensive training in 1993, three years had passed since the publication of *Narrative means to therapeutic ends*. In those three years, the potential of the narrative metaphor for therapy had been further expanded. A key paper by David Epston and Michael White (1990) had focused more thoroughly on possible applications of the rite of passage metaphor (Turner, 1967; van Gennep, 1960) and ways to 'consult your consultants': 'what distinguished consulting your consultants from any other "therapy" practice of its time was "consultation" from a "veteran" of the problem to a "sufferer" of the problem.' (D. Epston, personal communication, May 29, 2011; see also Marsten, Epston, & Johnson, 2011). This process was a key precedent for collective narrative practice.

Around the same time, Michael White (1991) wrote a substantial text, 'Deconstruction and therapy', which drew on Bourdieu (1988), Derrida (1981) and Jerome Bruner (1986) to provide more detailed examples of 'landscape of action' (M. White, 1991, p. 128) and 'landscape of consciousness' (1991, p. 131) questions and how these could contribute to the generation of alternative stories. And of course, 'Some thoughts on men's ways of being' (Dulwich Centre, 1992) had been published. Thanks to the generosity of Cheryl White, I left that first intensive with a copy of everything that had ever been written about 'reauthoring' or 'narrative therapy'! Many years later, as I have been revisiting this history, I have been relying on these same copies of the original early texts.

Each night, sitting in the youth hostel lounge, there was so much to think about. Given that I was not a therapist and never planned to work as one, I was particularly interested in how these reauthoring ideas could relate to broader projects. There seemed so many possibilities, as John McLeod (2007) described:

In social terms, traditional individualist psychological therapies operate as a kind of emotional 'sink' into which communal and interpersonal tensions can be absorbed. By contrast, narrative therapy has the capacity to channel the energy arising from individual troubles, and shape it into productive social action. In this work, the concept of narrative provides a bridge between the stories told by specific persons, and the dominant discourses and narratives within which we all collectively live our lives. (McLeod, 2007, p. 244)

It was this bridge that both fascinated and excited me. So too did the ways in which Dulwich Centre's 'community of ideas' was already engaged with a number of social projects.

The social projects

Cheryl White (2011) has described the ways in which the development of narrative therapy was intricately linked to broader social movements and social projects of the 1960s and 1970s:

We were of the times when social movements were challenging taken-for-granted authority in a range of areas. Initially, the focus was the Vietnam War and feminism. And then the focus changed. Along with many others, Michael [White] became determined to challenge and put forward alternatives to the taken-for-granted authorities within mental health services and psychiatry.

From the 1960s onwards, writers including Michel Foucault, Erving Goffman, R.D. Laing, Thomas Szasz, and Franco Basaglia began to critique routinely accepted practices within psychiatry and the influence of psychiatric understandings within society more generally. Consumer/survivor movements of those who had endured degradations within mental health institutions also began campaigning for change. We had seen a social movement stop a war, and another change the ways in which women and men relate to each other and to life. As people in many different countries became determined to alter the ways in which their societies responded to those in social and emotional distress, this became a passion in Michael's life. And it is this commitment that led to the development of what is now known as narrative therapy. (C. White, 2011, p. 159)

During my first week in Adelaide, I was introduced to three different social projects that Dulwich Centre was then involved with. Learning about these social projects was of equal significance to me as the ideas taught in the intensive. I will briefly describe the social projects I was introduced to during that week and discuss their implications.

Explorations of gender partnership: Social action in relation to gender justice

My first conversation with Cheryl White involved me mentioning that I was working with an organisation called Men Against Sexual Assault and Cheryl raising a number of brilliantly articulated questions and critiques about the politics and naming of such work. Two years later, a group of young men[7] who were also exploring ways of taking local social action in relation to men's violence travelled to Adelaide and the community of practitioners associated with Dulwich Centre opened their homes and lives to provide us with a context to further consider ways of addressing the very real harm caused by men's violence and by dominant constructions of masculinity (Flood, 1995; Kriewaldt, 1995).

The result of these conversations in Adelaide, and Michael White's intensive training, led me to reconfigure the work that I was involved with in prison and in schools. I was intrigued as to how reauthoring conversations could occur collectively, in non-therapeutic contexts, and in response to social issues of gender and violence (see Denborough, 1995a).

I had discovered that gender partnerships, of which I was now a part, could provide a context for the generation of new ideas and practices. I, for one, was profoundly appreciative that Taimalieutu Kiwi Tamasese had challenged and inspired Cheryl White to work with men in her own culture on issues of gender. While the shape, form and memberships of these gender partnerships have changed over the years, they remain central to collective narrative practices.[8]

An alternative community mental health project

On the Wednesday evening of that first intensive, an informal gathering of those involved in the Dulwich Centre alternative community mental health project took place. This project involved team members and community members working alongside each other to expose the tactics and effects of the 'voices and visions' (often referred to as the auditory and visual hallucinations of schizophrenia) experienced by the community members. The knowledges and skills of community members were honoured and built upon; ever-widening communities of reflection and support were created; and in the process many aspects of mainstream culture were called into question. During that first meeting, I was inspired to consider how the reauthoring practices I was learning in the intensive could reconfigure community responses to mental health concerns.

Four years on, the *Dulwich Centre Newsletter*, 'Companions on a journey' (Dulwich Centre Community Mental Health Project, 1997) was published. This included the first 'collective narrative documents' by the Power to Our Journeys group (Brigitte, Sue, Mem, & Veronika, 1997). Further development and refinement of ways in which collective narrative documents can be used in a range of contexts continues to be a key element of collective narrative practice (see Denborough, C. White, Claver, J. Freedman, & Combs, 2012).

Reclaiming our stories, reclaiming our lives: Responding to Aboriginal deaths in custody

The Royal Commission into Aboriginal Deaths in Custody handed down its report on 15 April 1991. This landmark commission was conducted by Elliot Johnson QC who had coincidentally owned and worked from 345 Carrington Street, Adelaide, which in 1991 was the location of Dulwich Centre. Recommendation 5 of the Royal Commission stated:

> That governments, recognising the trauma and pain suffered by relatives, kin and friends of those who died in custody, give sympathetic support to requests to provide funds or services to enable counselling to be offered to these people. (Australian Royal Commission into Aboriginal Deaths in Custody & Johnston, 1998)

In response, Tim Agius, the director of the Aboriginal Health Council of South Australia, was determined to provide some sort of counselling response to Aboriginal families who had lost loved ones in custody. Most significantly, he was determined to find or develop a culturally appropriate response to grief caused by injustice. This endeavour led him to consult with Dulwich Centre and these collaborations led to a gathering for all Aboriginal families from South Australia who had lost a family member in custody. This gathering was shaped by narrative ideas and was documented in 'Reclaiming our stories, reclaiming our lives' (Aboriginal Health Council, 1995).

The gathering was held at Camp Coorong and participants identified a number of aspects of the event as particularly helpful, including:

Naming injustice: Aboriginal people were able to identify the 'dominant story', which was about personal guilt and inadequacy, and rename it as injustice and oppression. The freedom to use words 'murder' and 'racism', and to publicly name their experiences of injustice, was experienced as profoundly freeing.

Listening teams: The practice of using 'listening teams' in which members of the counselling team formed an audience to Aboriginal people's stories, and then reflected upon what they had heard. A number of Aboriginal people commented that hearing their own stories reflected back in this way enabled them to see themselves differently, and to reclaim a pride in who they were. It also allowed them to recognise the remarkable strengths that they had demonstrated in surviving in the face of so much injustice. As one participant said about the listening groups, 'This reclaims the strengths of Aboriginal culture. Aboriginal culture has always had this. This has reiterated it, rejuvenated it. This is going on every day really around people's kitchen tables – so all you are doing now is going much wider and getting back to our culture.'

The 'journey' metaphor: The narrative approach makes considerable use of the 'journey' metaphor. Moving from dominant stories about one's life to preferred stories is like making a journey from one identity to another. The provision of metaphoric 'maps' of the sorts of experiences, feelings and pitfalls that can happen on this journey by other people who have already made it, can play an important part in enabling people to move forward in their lives … A number of Aboriginal people commented on the usefulness of the journey metaphor. (Aboriginal Health Council, 1995, pp. 19–20)

This event at Camp Coorong was the first narrative community gathering. Its approach was again the result of partnerships, as Michael White (2003) described:

I would like to acknowledge the contributions of Tim Agius and Barbara Wingard to our first explorations of the relevance of narrative practices in working with communities. The foundation of these first explorations was Tim's unwavering vision of a community-wide gathering that would provide a healing context for Aboriginal families of South Australia that had lost a member through death in jail or prison. The spirit and wisdom that Tim and Barbara then brought to this initiative and so willingly shared with the members of our team sustained us in so many ways. (M. White, 2003, p. 53)

Although I was only involved in a very peripheral way in the Camp Coorong gathering (I took part in early consultative conversations about prisons), this project profoundly influenced my own work. This project provided the blueprint for further narrative gatherings in which I played a part. These gatherings involved Aboriginal communities in Narrandera and Bowraville, NSW (Denborough, 2002a); people with a HIV-positive diagnosis and workers within the HIV sector (Dulwich Centre, 2000); and gatherings in relation to mental health (ACT Mental Health Consumers Network & Dulwich Centre, 2003; South Australian Council of Social Service & Dulwich Centre, 1995).

It was during these gatherings that a form of narrative community songwriting emerged (Denborough, 2002b, 2008) and we discovered ways in which songs can contribute powerful outsider-witness responses (M. White, 2000). While I remain devoted to the written word, particularly its rigour, its capacity to record all that is spoken, the ways in which drafts can be shared and collectively edited, and its intimate characteristics (how it speaks to each individual who reads it), songs can be sung together in ways that the written word cannot. In some contexts, the written word is not accessible to all, whereas songs and music can include most people in any community. And perhaps most significantly, with a good melody, songs can remain in one's mind, available for instant recall in a way that the written word cannot.[9]

The 'Reclaiming our stories, reclaiming our lives' project heralded the beginning of partnerships between Dulwich Centre, Tim Agius and Barbara Wingard, which remain to this day and continue to influence work within Aboriginal communities.

On the completion of 'Reclaiming our stories, reclaiming our lives', Dulwich Centre decided to focus further on the role of prisons in the perpetuation of injustice, to investigate ways of looking 'beyond the prison', and to 'gather dreams of freedom' from Australia, New Zealand, the USA and Canada. I was 25 at the time and this research turned out to be life-changing (Denborough, 1995b):

At first glance, the current culture of imprisonment appears to be growing stronger. Increasing numbers of men and women are being locked away, for longer and longer sentences, and in newer and larger prisons. And yet ... there are rich alternative traditions upon which to build, both here in this country and elsewhere.

My mind flashes to songs deep within prison walls, to the daily acts of resistance, to those who care, to those who dare to speak, to those who survive another day marked off on a calendar. In concert with these people are Indigenous Australians, vocal in their resistance to deaths in custody and imprisonment as a tool of colonisation. From here to the circles of the Yukon, to marae justice, to the creation of new courtrooms and new ways of working, there are powerful foundations on which to build. The communities most affected by imprisonment seem to be lighting new ways forward, creating the possibility of weeding out notions of punishment from our beings, from our institutions of degradation, and from our cities.

This country was invaded to become a prison, not only for the Indigenous Peoples, but also for the poor of Britain. Now, over two hundred years after this country was invaded to become a prison, cracks are beginning to appear in the culture of imprisonment, cracks caused by generations of protest. (Denborough, 1996, p. 221)

When the book *Beyond the prison: Gathering dreams of freedom* (Denborough, 1996) was complete, I moved to Adelaide and began to work behind the scenes in the flourishing 'community of ideas' (C. White & Denborough, 2005) of Dulwich Centre Publications.

Dulwich Centre Publications: A community of ideas

Since the 17th century, magazines have been a peculiarly modern device for bringing a public space into existence. Like a town meeting, a magazine enables people to be in each other's company by sharing talk about matters that concern them. And it is through talking with others that most of us start to make some sense of the world, and begin to discover who we are and what we think. (Denneny, 1984, p. 13)

Influenced by her studies of anthropology and her participation in the women's liberation movement, Cheryl White founded Dulwich Centre Publications with a particular ethos. She drew her inspiration from feminism and from the work of alternative community publishers such as Michael Denneny, the editor of the gay male magazine, *Christopher Street*, who described a particular publishing aim: '*Christopher Street* has never tried to develop a party line; we always thought our task was to open a space, a forum, where the developing gay culture could manifest and experience itself' (Denneny, 1984, p. 13). Although the context for Dulwich Centre Publications was very different from gay New York, the publishing aim was similar. In this case, how to open space and forums where a developing 'culture' of non-pathologising practice could experience and manifest itself.

It is worth mentioning that the Dulwich Centre Publications actually began as a series of forums entitled 'Friday Afternoons at Dulwich':[10]

Twenty years ago, here in Adelaide, some therapists began to share their work in free forums that involved short presentations on particular ideas and then rigorous debate and discussion ... these forums ... were open to anyone interested in the particular topic being addressed. There was so much energy and interest in the presentations that it seemed a good idea to write these down and a small news-sheet was developed for this purpose. Links were generated between a range of local practitioners and these first news-sheets were simply a way to continue the conversations. Over time, people from other places requested copies of the news-sheets and it gradually turned into a journal. Interest in the ideas continued to grow and, in 1989, Dulwich Centre Publications published its first book, *Literate Means to Therapeutic Ends*, by David Epston and Michael White. (C. White & Denborough, 2005, p. 4)

In the early days, there were very few places where emerging 'narrative therapy papers' could be published. A number of early papers by Michael White, now seen as breakthrough papers and referred to by practitioners throughout the world, had been rejected by other publishers and only saw the light of day due to Dulwich Centre Publications. Throughout its history, Dulwich Centre Publications has consistently expanded the boundaries of what is thought to be 'appropriate' to therapists. For instance, the publication of 'Reclaiming our stories, reclaiming our lives' (Aboriginal Health Council of South Australia, 1995), about responding to Aboriginal families who had lost a family member to a death in custody, resulted in the loss of a third of subscribers to the *Dulwich Centre Newsletter*.[11] Sixteen years later, a conference on Aboriginal health heralded it as a landmark publication.[12]

Establishing a feminist-informed publishing house dedicated to the generation and sustenance of a community of ideas required the development of alternative review processes, deliberate efforts to ensure gender parity of authors, and a continual investment to ensure that the voices of those rarely heard could inform discussions in the emerging field of narrative therapy and community work. My job, as staff writer, was to research and document hopeful stories of work that would be of interest to readers. There was an aspiration that each publication would not simply confirm what was already known, but instead lead practitioners to engage with new possibilities for the narrative metaphor in therapy and community work.

Told in the 'third voice'

Sometimes the work of an editor is to support the writing projects of authors. At other times, it involves conducting interviews and then publishing these. But often, at Dulwich Centre Publications, we interview practitioners and/or community members and then write up these interviews in the voice of the interview subject. The interviewer is active in asking questions to generate rich descriptions of the ideas, skills and knowledges of the interview subject, and the stories are written to include all the information that is generated through the conversation. In our experience, this creates a far richer telling than would be possible if the person were to write up their own work or if the story remained in interview format – particularly when an interview subject's preferred language is not English.

This method of working and documenting can be likened to the generation of the 'third voice' that Barbara Myerhoff, the American anthropologist, was exploring in the later years of her life. As Marc Kaminsky (1992a) explains, Barbara Myerhoff 'wished to find a way of editing the tales so that everything she knew about them would be "invisibly" embedded in the tales, through the editing: the tales would be presented without … [any] framing discourse' (1992a, p. 13). Of course, these practices require processes of accountability and partnership to ensure that interview subjects have control over how they and their 'knowledge' are represented. A number of 'third voice' publishing projects have been highly influential in the development of collective narrative practices.

Collective externalising conversations / narrative theatre

In the mid-1990s, Yvonne Sliep and the CARE Counsellors of Malawi (Sliep & CARE Counsellors, 1996) were responding to the HIV/AIDS epidemic in rural Malawi. Local health workers applied the narrative concept of 'externalising problems' (see Roth & Epston, 1996) in theatrical ways. Community members were invited to interview health workers who played the roles of 'Mr AIDS' and 'Mrs CARE' (representing Community Action Renders Enablement). These 'collective externalising conversations' then provided the opening for conversations in the villages between older men, older women, younger men and younger women as they tried to find ways to build upon the skills, knowledges, and traditions of the community. Yvonne Sliep has since gone on to further develop forms of narrative theatre (Sliep, 2005; Sliep, Weingarten, & Gilbert, 2004). Aboriginal health worker Barbara Wingard has developed her own forms of collective externalising conversations in response to diabetes ('sugar'), grief (Wingard, 1996a, 1996b) and lateral violence (Wingard, 2010). Others have taken this approach into school contexts (McMenamin, 1999).

Telling our stories in ways that make us stronger

Perhaps the most significant 'third voice' publishing process involved a writing partnership with Aunty Barbara Wingard and Jane Lester, which resulted in the publication of *Telling our stories in ways that make us stronger* (Wingard & Lester, 2001). This beautiful book contains stories from Aunty Barbara and Jane about their work, their lives, the histories of Australia and their own forms of narrative practice. My involvement in the writing partnership was powerfully significant to me, so much so that it has altered the ways in which I understand my own family histories. When Jane Lester (2001) presented a keynote address, 'Coming home: Voices of the day' at the third International Narrative Therapy and Community Work Conference, I presented alongside her:

Three years ago, I first spoke with Jane and learnt of her meticulous searching and how she was able to link the stories of her family with the history of this country. I was quite overcome at both the sorrow and the extraordinary reclamation of which she spoke. As I reflected on how little I knew of my own family histories, and how they might be linked to events in this nation's past, I made a quiet vow to myself. I vowed that I would trace the histories of my family in the hope that in future conversations with Jane and others, the stories I discovered could in some way be linked and shared. It was Jane's generosity of spirit that started me on a journey through family history that has led me to be speaking here this morning.

Just as Jane offered stories of family this morning, I would like to do similarly. But of course the stories of my family are very different. My father was not forcibly removed from his family and nor were his siblings or his cousins. In fact, in many ways, the histories I wish to speak about could not be more different. I wish to speak about my relationship to the life of my great-great-grandfather on my mother's side. His name was Samuel Griffith. He was instrumental in drafting the Australian Constitution and went on to become the first Chief Justice of this country. He is considered one of the founding fathers of Federation, the centenary of which is being celebrated in Australia this year. In some ways, my search to understand the life of Samuel Griffith could not be more different than the search Jane spoke of earlier. But there are some similarities. I would not be alive if it were not for Samuel Griffith, and my search to understand his life is changing the ways in which I understand my own. I have learnt largely through my conversations with Indigenous Australians something of the importance of honouring heritage, or respecting those who lived lives dedicated to us – their children, grandchildren, great-grandchildren. But honouring ancestry is a complex process when your family histories are interwoven with the dispossession of others. One side of my Australian ancestry were involved in literally dispossessing Aboriginal people of their land in northern Queensland. Another side was instrumental in crafting a constitution which in some ways legalised this dispossession. To quote Andrea Rieniets (1995): 'What do you do when you find that your family tree has been replanted in someone else's yard?' That is the question with which I and so many other non-Indigenous Australians are currently grappling.

In some ways, it seems to me that the process of tracing history involves speaking across time and across generations. And so in preparing for this morning I decided it might be most appropriate to try to write Samuel Griffith a letter. I'd like to share that letter with you if that's okay. (Denborough, 2001, p. 7)

I will not include this letter here, but I do wish to reiterate that the writing partnerships associated with the book *Telling our stories in ways that make us stronger* created far more than a text. They also contributed to new ways for all of us involved to understand our lives, our relationships and our families in this country.

Family therapy: exploring the field's past, present and possible futures

Speaking of families, narrative therapy's 'family of origin' was the field of family therapy. In 2001, in order to honour this history, Dulwich Centre Publications embarked on a project to interview a wide range of leading family therapists. The idea was to bring together in one text many different practitioners' perspectives on the histories of family therapy, the work that people were currently engaged in, and their hopes for the future of family therapy.

As I had not been a part of the field of family therapy, and had come to know it only through my engagement with narrative practice, I needed to undertake considerable research prior to interviewing, among others: Insoo Kim Berg, Salvador Minuchin, Monica McGoldrick, Gianfranco Cecchin, Kerrie James, Kenneth V. Hardy, Olga Silverstein, Tom Andersen, Peggy Papp, Karl Tomm, Michael White, Peggy Penn, Lynn Hoffman, David Epston, Warihi Campbell, Taimalieutu Kiwi Tamasese and Charles Waldegrave.

Being introduced to these people, their stories and their histories, changed my understanding of narrative practice. I could now locate certain narrative philosophies of practice within wider family therapy traditions. For instance, the following principles (see White, 2001b), which all inform narrative practice, can be linked to earlier developments within the field of family therapy:

- considering identity as something that is achieved in relationship with others rather than something that derives from 'human nature'

- understanding people's problems within the wider contexts of their lives rather than locating problems within individuals

- committing to meet with families and other networks and communities of people to address the problems in their lives (rather than considering individual therapy as the only form of legitimate interaction between therapist and client)

- emphasising how the renegotiation of people's identities occurs within the context of their interactions with others

- conceptualising therapy as a process of questioning

- proposing an ethic of transparency in that the work of therapists should be made visible through live interviews and videos.

Making narrative ideas accessible to a wide readership

One further publishing project is also relevant to mention here. Dulwich Centre Publications has been determined to make narrative therapy ideas accessible to as wide a readership as possible. This involved publishing the introductory text *What is narrative therapy? An easy-to-read introduction* (A. Morgan, 2000) and its companion, *Narrative therapy: Responding to your questions* (Russell & Carey, 2004). Both these books were the result of significant collaborations. The hope of making narrative ideas accessible to a wide readership was also influential in Michael White writing the book *Maps of narrative practice* (2007). The reason I mention this broader publishing project here is that it has informed how publications about collective narrative practice have been written – in the hope that they will be accessible to a wide audience.

ond neoliberal fatalism: Meeting Paulo Freire

The work of Paulo Freire (1973, 1994, 1999; Freire & Macebo, 1987) has inspired approaches to popular education and community work throughout Brazil and across the world. In 1997, while in Brazil to document the work of the Association of Street People (Varanda, 1999), Cheryl White and I conducted what was to be Paulo Freire's final interview (Freire, 1999). Within it, Freire railed against the ways in which the privileged in the world routinely look for solutions in the wrong places and then, when they cannot find the solutions there, they feel despair, and become convinced that broader change is not possible and therefore not worth aspiring to or acting towards. He named this phenomenon 'neo-liberal fatalism' (Freire, 1999) and believed it was perhaps the greatest obstacle we faced.

These words about neoliberalism and the politics of despair were highly significant and challenging to me. I have known despair at different times in my life: despair about whether broader social change is really possible, despair about how people treat people. Paulo Freire had also lived a life in which he had known despair. His pedagogy of hope (1994) was not born of simple optimism. It was a hope that knew despair and was stronger for this knowledge.

The interview with Freire and his challenge within it to shape our lives and work in ways that prioritise contributing to broader social change have contributed significantly to the development of collective narrative practice (see Denborough, 2008, p. xi). In fact, collective narrative practice is shaped by the question: How can we respond to stories of social suffering in ways that not only alleviate individual sorrow, but also enable and sustain local social action to address the broader injustices, violence and abuses?

Community responses to violence and harassment

Seeking creative and effective ways of preventing and responding to violence has also been a longstanding commitment of Dulwich Centre Publications (Durrant & C. White, 1990; Jenkins, 1990). Between

1998 and 2002, we published a number of projects to further articulate how narrative practices can inform collective responses to violence. These included documenting the work of: Silent Too Long – a group of women survivors of childhood sexual (Silent Too Long, 1998, 2000, 2001); WOWSAFE – a group of women survivors of domestic violence (WOWSAFE, 2002); the Anti-harassment Team of Selwyn College in New Zealand (Selwyn College, Lewis, & Cheshire, 1998); and work within Latino communities in California attempting to prevent domestic violence and create respectful relationships in culturally resonant ways (Colorado, Montgomery, & Tovar, 2003). More recent texts have also considered multicultural responses to gendered violence (Yuen & C. White, 2007).

Enabling people to become guardians of their own health – America Bracho

Inspired by the work of Paulo Freire, America Bracho's work with Latino Health Access in Orange County, California, has reconfigured a physical health service (providing services in relation to diabetes, heart disease and HIV/AIDS) to become an 'institute of participation' (Bracho & Latino Health Access, 2000, p. 4):

It is our responsibility to provide mechanisms in a sensitive way that enable people to demonstrate, to perform their caring. It is our responsibility to notice and enquire about the assets, talents and skills of the community and to provide contexts by which the people we are working with can take actions to contribute towards the accomplishment of their hopes, aims and dreams. (Bracho & Latino Health Access, 2000, p. 7)

If it is possible to transform a physical health service in this way, could it also be possible to similarly reconfigure responses to mental health and/or responses to trauma? Influenced by the work of Latino Health Access, Dulwich Centre Foundation's use of collective narrative practices continues to explore this question.

Conferences as community gatherings: Honouring histories, cultural protocols and partnerships

Being a part of the Dulwich Centre conference organising team from 1999 onwards has brought its own challenges and learnings which have been significant in the development of collective narrative practice. Dulwich Centre Publications conceptualises its conferences as 'community events' and this involves considerations of honouring histories, cultural protocols and partnerships (C. White & Denborough, 2005).

The work of Taimalieutu Kiwi Tamasese, Flora Tuhaka, Warihi Campbell and Charles Waldegrave of the Just Therapy Team of New Zealand (Waldegrave, 1990; Waldegrave, Tamasese, Tuhaka, & Campbell, 2003), and partnerships with Aboriginal Australian colleagues Barbara Wingard and Tim Agius, have transformed our understandings of what it means to honour the histories of the land on which a conference is to take place, how to welcome participants to such an event, and how to respond to cultural complexities and historic and current injustice through partnership.

In relation to the co-hosting of conferences, these partnerships have involved travelling with African-American colleagues Makungu Akinyela and Vanessa Jackson to visit the Cape Coast slave castles of Ghana (Amemasor, 2002) prior to holding an event in Atlanta, Georgia. They have involved Patrick Moss and Julie Moss travelling hundreds and hundreds of miles with a van load of young men from the Keetowah Band of the Cherokee to open this same conference. They have involved indigenous traditional healers from different parts of the state of Oaxaca, Mexico, welcoming participants and offering consultations during the sixth International Narrative Therapy and Community Work Conference.[13]

These experiences, partnerships and relationships in some ways laid the groundwork for the cross-cultural inventions of collective narrative practices which I will describe in the next section.

The emergence of collective narrative practice

Having outlined a range of projects in which narrative therapy ideas and principles were put to work outside a counselling context from the early 1990s, I now wish to describe how, over the past decade, a number of factors have seen the emergence of a field which has come to be known as collective narrative practice. This field endeavours to build on the histories described above and to put them to use in responding to situations of hardship and trauma in contexts where counselling or therapy is either not culturally resonant or not possible. I will briefly outline a number of factors that coalesced in order to lead to the generation of this field.

A renewed focus on responding to hardship and trauma

From 2003 onwards, Dulwich Centre started to focus more attention on narrative responses to trauma. This coincided with being invited to visit and work with Palestinian therapists working at the Treatment and Rehabilitation Centre for Victims of Torture and Trauma (TRC) based in Ramallah, Palestine. The presentation that Michael White gave at the TRC in October 2003 was recorded. In consultation with those present, it was decided that it would be helpful to have this presentation transcribed, edited and then translated into Arabic to be made available to Arabic-speaking workers in Palestine and elsewhere. This paper, 'Working with people who are suffering the consequences of multiple trauma: A narrative perspective' (M. White, 2004b) emphasised the priority to be given to the redevelopment and reinvigoration of a 'sense of myself' when working with people who have been subject to trauma. It described how this can be achieved through the use of definitional ceremony structures, outsider-witness practices and reauthoring conversations. And the last section of the paper discussed the work of memory theorists and its relevance to work with people who have experienced trauma. This approach has proved influential, and Michael White gave a keynote on a related theme at the fourth International Narrative Therapy and Community Work Conference.[14] He also taught a number of five-day special intensives on narrative responses to trauma and presented internationally on this topic.

At the same time as Michael White was teaching about responses trauma, we were researching and documenting examples of the use of narrative practices in responding to trauma in Bangladesh, Israel, South Africa, USA, UK and Sri Lanka (see Dulwich Centre, 2005a, 2005b). I was also creating a framework for receiving and documenting testimonies of trauma (Denborough, 2005) and initiating a project to respond to sexual violence within prisons (Denborough & Preventing Prisoner Rape Project, 2005). These new developments were compiled into a book, *Trauma: Narrative responses to traumatic experience* (Denborough, 2006). The ideas in this book have provided the intellectual foundation for a range of collective projects responding to traumatic experience within communities in Australia, Bosnia, Rwanda, Palestine, Uganda and elsewhere.

Invitations (demands!) to teach and collaborate across cultures

The second development that took place was a curious one. Suddenly, while Cheryl White and I were visiting various places in order to research and document local initiatives, we were asked to teach about the use of narrative practices. We would routinely turn down these invitations and explain that we were actually interested in what local practitioners were doing in response to the local context and local dilemmas. A part of our refusal was our determination to try to avoid imposing narrative approaches that had been developed in Australia and New Zealand on very different cultural contexts. And yet, suddenly, the invitations to teach became more demanding. I vividly recall colleagues in Bangladesh, India and in Palestine virtually insisting that we were withholding knowledge and experience from them and that they expected us to teach. An afternoon in Nablus, Palestine, was a particular turning point. We arrived with pen and paper in order to document local initiatives, and discovered a room set out with 20 chairs and were told that the training we were to provide was to start in 20 minutes! A similar situation took place in a drug rehabilitation centre in India. With nothing prepared to teach, these contexts required us to:

- develop forms of teaching that used examples of practice that were resonant with local contexts; this often meant examples that did not involve one-on-one counselling

- develop pedagogies that demonstrated the use of narrative practices, using the experiences of local practitioners, but without in any way putting individuals on the spot; for instance, without conducting individual interviews or role-plays.

A key development in relation to collective narrative documentation occurred while teaching in Nablus, Palestine. Seeking ways to ensure that the teaching was relevant to local practitioners who themselves were living and working under military occupation, I developed a collective narrative document from their words and stories: 'Dealing with life under occupation: The special skills and knowledges that sustain the workers of Nablus' (Denborough, 2008, p. 32). This was then retold/performed. The process proved to be a significant learning experience for all involved and has subsequently became a routine element of collective narrative practice training.

Around the same time, two other key developments occurred that involved invitations to generate narrative methodologies that could be used beyond the counselling room to respond to profound hardship and social suffering.

The Tree of Life and the Team of Life: Collective narrative methodologies

Ncazelo Ncube-Mlilo is a Zimbabwean practitioner who in 2005 was working with REPSSI, an organisation based in South Africa that builds capacity in relation to working with vulnerable children throughout southern and eastern Africa. Through Ncazelo Ncube's interest in narrative ideas, REPSSI and Dulwich Centre were involved in a partnership that saw teams from Dulwich Centre visit Zimbabwe in 2005 and Uganda in 2006. These visits had dual purposes. The first purpose was for the Dulwich Centre team,[15] principally Michael White, to provide training in narrative therapy to a range of African practitioners. The second purpose of the visit to Zimbabwe was a request from Ncazelo Ncube-Mlilo for me to develop a form of narrative practice that could be used with vulnerable children in collective contexts. The result of our collaboration was the Tree of Life (Denborough, 2008; Ncube, 2006): the first collective narrative methodology based on a metaphor drawn from local folklore. The Tree of Life is discussed in Chapter 3. The second purpose of the visit to Uganda was to develop a way of working with former child soldiers. It was in this context that I developed the Team of Life methodology (Denborough, 2008).

Linking storylines between Aboriginal communities

At around the same time as our work in Africa, Dulwich Centre was invited by Barry Sullivan and Relationships Australia to be involved in a suicide prevention project with a number of Aboriginal communities in the Northern Territory. It soon became clear to Barbara Wingard, Cheryl White and myself (who together were leading the Dulwich Centre team[16]) that a new approach would need to be developed for this particular context. This new approach was described in the paper 'Linking stories and initiatives: A narrative approach to working with the skills and knowledge of communities':

Within any community that is facing difficult times, community members will be responding to these difficulties, they will be taking whatever action is possible, in their own ways, based on particular skills and knowledges, to try to address the effects of the problem(s) on their lives and the lives of those they love and care about. These initiatives may not currently be widely recognised, and they may not in themselves be enough to overcome all that is presently facing the community. These initiatives are, however, highly significant. Making it possible for community members to identify these initiatives, to richly describe them so that the skills and knowledges implicit within them become more visible to themselves and to others, and to trace the history of these skills and knowledges so that the ways these are linked to local culture are understood, can strengthen these initiatives in ways that make further action possible.

Finding audiences to witness stories about these initiatives is a next step. If richly described stories of community initiatives are witnessed and responded to by those in other communities facing similar difficulties, if messages can be sent back and forth, then support and a sense of solidarity can be generated. Those community members already taking action can be powerfully supported in this process, while others can be inspired to join in. The documentation, circulation and celebration of community skills and knowledge can, in time, take on a life of its own.

This paper describes an approach to community work that requires engagement with at least two communities at a time, as each community is invited to become an outsider witness to the stories of the other. This form of community engagement is characterised by a criss-crossing exchange of stories and messages. (Denborough, Koolmatrie, Mununggirritj, Marika, Dhurrkay, & Yunupingu, 2006, p. 20)

This new narrative approach that involves working with two communities at a time has also influenced the ways in which survivors of the genocide in Rwanda have been linked with Jewish descendants of Holocaust survivors. More recently, it shaped the projects with diverse groups of young people that were described in Part I of this book.

Dulwich Centre Foundation and the challenges for collective narrative practice

The final factor that sparked a concerted effort to develop further collective narrative practices came in 2006, when Michael White, Cheryl White and I visited Rwanda and made contact with Kaboyi Benoit, who at that time was the executive secretary of Ibuka, the national genocide survivors association (Benoit, 2007). Sitting at the top of 'Hotel Rwanda'

(Hôtel des Mille Collines), we decided that we would form the Dulwich Centre Institute of Collective Practice (which in time became Dulwich Centre Foundation) in order to respond to the following questions and challenges:

- In contexts where one-on-one counselling is not possible or culturally appropriate, how can narrative approaches be used to assist people who are experiencing hardship?

- Where resources are scarce, how can we develop narrative approaches that can be put into practice by dedicated community people; approaches that can be engaged with beyond the professional world?

- How can narrative approaches be made relevant to contexts of profound collective social suffering such as the genocide in Rwanda and the military occupation of Palestine?

- In responding to stories of social suffering, how can our work contribute to 'social movement'?

- As we respond to these questions, how can we minimise the possibilities of participating in psychological colonisation? (see Arulampalam, et al., 2006; Pupavac, 2001, 2002a, 2002b, 2006; Tamasese, 2002a; Watters, 2010).

Michael White's death at an early age in 2008 was a tragic loss for the field. The legacies of his work, however, live on in many different ways and places. For instance, using Michael's ideas as our foundation, and the questions above as our challenge, new forms of collective narrative practice have emerged. So too have new ways of theorising our roles as practitioners:

Our first task ... is to develop ways of working that unearth (and then richly describe) the skills and knowledges of those who have experienced trauma and hardship. Our second task is to 'enable contribution' ... People enduring significant hardship are often seen to be requiring 'help', 'healing', 'therapy', or 'psychosocial support' and it is often assumed that this 'help' is to be provided through professional services. But perhaps something quite different is required. Perhaps what is required is for contexts to be created in which individuals and communities who are going through hard times can make contributions to the lives of others who are going through similar difficulties. (Denborough, 2008, pp. 1–4)

Closing words

This chapter has traced my journey through the history of ideas, practices and partnerships that led to the development of narrative therapy, and the challenges and invitations that have contributed to the development of collective narrative practice. In doing so, I hope it has provided a historical foundation for this emerging field.

In excavating this foundation, I have traversed the intellectual roots of narrative therapy – writings from the interpretive turn in anthropology and the early papers of Michael White and David Epston – in relation to six key aspects of narrative therapy:

- placing personal problems back into the realm of culture and history: externalising

- the narrative metaphor and narrative practice

- counter documents and therapeutic letters

- the significance of partnerships

- an anthropology of problems and archiving alternative knowledges

- folk psychology and performed identity.

And yet, the histories that inform collective narrative practice are not only intellectual, so I have also included stories of the social projects and partnerships that have been critical along the way.

At the beginning of this chapter, I described how at 23 I was struggling to work out how to respond to what were, for me, two relatively recent discoveries: that my European family tree had been 'replanted in someone else's yard' (Rieniets, 1995), namely the yard belonging to Aboriginal Australia. And the harm that people of my gender (men) had done and were continuing to do to women, to children and to other men.

Twenty-five years on, if I were to attempt to describe how I now respond to these questions, it would be the word 'partnership'. As a white, middle-class Australian man, the only way I can hope to make any contribution to redressing the effects of gender injustice, racial injustice, or the effects of war and social suffering, is through the formation of meaningful and lasting partnerships with those most affected by these injustices. Just as collective narrative practices have developed through partnerships, their future will depend on them.[17]

Looking back, the development of collective narrative practices has been quite a journey. If I were to nominate its starting point, it would be a conversation in November 2006 with Cheryl White and Michael White at the Hôtel des Mille Collines looking over Rwanda, the land of a thousand hills. The challenges we were seeking to respond to during that conversation in Rwanda remain just as significant today. In writing this book, however, I have come to more fully appreciate the distances and territories we have travelled since then, the learnings that have accrued, and possible future explorations. I have also come to a much greater understanding of the histories we are building upon and all those who are accompanying us along the way.

Let the adventures continue …

Notes

1. This chapter was written prior to Cheryl White's (2016) landmark publication *A memory book for the field of narrative practice*. I highly recommend this social history text to anyone who is interested in the diverse contributions that led to the development of narrative therapy. Other histories of narrative therapy include Beels (2001, 2009), Chamberlain (2004, 2011), Denborough (2009), Epston (2011), Madigan (2011) and C. White (2009).

2. From a song by Andrea Rieniets (1995).

3. Other key collaborators in MASA at this time were David Newman, Mark D'Astoli and Mark Trudinger.

4. This paper was written after David Epston and Michael White spent time working together in Adelaide in August 1985.

5. For more information about this development see Epston (2011).

6. See www.narrativeapproaches.com/resources/anorexia-bulimia-archives-of-resistance/

7. These included David Newman, Michael Flood, Ben Pennings, Mark D'Astoli and Mark Trudinger.

8. To read collective documents to support initiatives in relation to gender-based violence in Palestine, contact Dulwich Centre Foundation c/o dulwich@dulwichcentre.com.au

9. Examples of such songs can be heard at: www.dulwichcentre.com.au/songs.html

10. Cheryl White has reinstated Friday Afternoons at Dulwich, this time online at dulwichcentre.com.au/category/friday-afternoons/

11. Cheryl White, personal communication, May 3, 2011.

12. Healing our way: Cultural approaches to working with Aboriginal families and communities impacted by the trauma of violence, March 1–2, 2011. Organised by Family Worker Training, NSW (www.fwtdp.org.au)

13. Lynn Tron's contributions to this process were invaluable.

14. An extract from this keynote presentation was published in C. White (2011).

15. The team in Zimbabwe consisted of Michael White, Cheryl White, Shona Russell and David Denborough. The team in Uganda consisted of Michael White, Cheryl White, Eileen Hurley and David Denborough.

16. This team also included Carolynanha Johnson, Shona Russell, Sue Mitchell and Barry Sullivan.

17. I wish to acknowledge here the following longer-term partnerships through which my engagement with collective narrative practices has emerged:
   - in relation to issues of gender: with Cheryl White and Mary Heath
   - in relation to considerations of culture: with Taimalieutu Kiwi Tamasese and Charles Waldegrave of the Just Therapy Team
   - in relation to Aboriginal/non-Aboriginal relations: with Aunty Barbara Wingard.

REFERENCES

Aboriginal Health Council of South Australia. (1995). Reclaiming our stories, reclaiming our lives. *Dulwich Centre Newsletter, 1*, 1–40.

Abu-Rayyan, N. (2014). The seasons of life: Ex-detainees reclaiming their lives. In Treatment and Rehabilitation Centre for Victims of Torture & Dulwich Centre Foundation International, *Responding to trauma that is not past: Strengthening stories of survival and resistance – An Arabic narrative therapy handbook* (pp. 28–31). Adelaide, Australia: Dulwich Centre Publications.

Abu-Rayyan, N. M. (2009). Seasons of Life: Ex-detainees reclaiming their lives. *International Journal of Narrative Practice and Community Work*, (2), 24–40.

Acharya, B. (2010). Narrative foundations and social justice. *International Journal of Narrative Therapy and Community Work*, (3), 33–39.

ACT Mental Health Consumers Network & Dulwich Centre. (2003). These are not ordinary lives: The report of a mental health community gathering. *International Journal of Narrative Therapy and Community Work*, (3), 29–49.

Adams, F., & Horton, M. (1975). *Unearthing seeds of fire: The idea of Highlander*. Winston-Salem, NC: Blair.

Adorno, T. (with Leppert, R.). (1992). *Essays on music* (S. H. Gillespie, Trans). Berkeley: University of California Press.

Alinsky, S. D. (1971). *Rules for radicals: A practical primer for realistic radicals*. New York, NY: Random House.

Allen, P. (1970). *Free Space: A perspective on the small group in women's liberation*. Washington, NJ: Times Change Press.

Amemasor, J. A. (2002). Opening the door of return. *International Journal of Narrative Therapy and Community Work*, (2), 60–63.

Appadurai, A. (2004). The capacity to aspire: Culture and the terms of recognition. In V. Rao & M. Walton (Eds.), *Culture and public action* (pp. 59–84). Stanford, CA: Stanford University Press.

Arendt, H. (1994). We refugees. In M. Robinson (Ed.), *Altogether elsewhere: Writers on exile* (pp. 111–119). Boston, MA: Faber. (Original work published 1943)

Arulampalam, S., Perera, L., de Mel, S., White, C., & Denborough, D. (2006). Avoiding psychological colonisation: Stories from Sri Lanka – responding to the tsunami. In D. Denborough (Ed.), *Trauma: Narrative responses to traumatic experience* (pp. 87–102). Adelaide, Australia: Dulwich Centre Publications.

Australian Royal Commission into Aboriginal Deaths in Custody & Johnston, E. (1998). *National Report* (Vol. 5). Retrieved from www.austlii.edu.au/au/other/IndigLRes/rciadic/national/vol5/5. html#Heading7

Bachelard, G. (1969). *The poetics of space*. Boston, MA: Beacon.

Bal, M. (2008). Visual narrativity. In D. Herman, M. Jahn, & M. Ryan (Eds.), *Routledge encyclopedia of narrative theory* (pp. 629–633). New York, NY: Routledge.

Baum, S., & Shaw, H. (2015). The tree of life methodology used as a group intervention for people with learning disabilities. *The Bulletin, 13*(1), 14–19.

Beels, C. (2001). *A different story: The rise of narrative in psychotherapy*. Phoenix, AZ: Zeig, Tucker and Theisen.

Beels, C. (2009). Some historical conditions of narrative work. *Family Process, 48*(3), 363–378.

Bellah, R. M., Madsen, R., Sullivan, W. M., Swidler, A., & Tipton, S. M. (1985). *Habits of the heart: Individualism and commitment in American life*. Berkeley: University of California Press.

Benoit, K. (2007). A small light as we walk this long road: The work of Ibuka. *International Journal of Narrative Therapy and Community Work,* (1), 47–50.

Benson, C. (2001). *The cultural psychology of self: Place, morality and art in the human world*. London, England: Routledge.

Billig, M., Condors, S., Edwards, D., Gane, M., Middleton, D., & Radley, A. (1988). *Ideological dilemmas: A social psychology of everyday thinking*. London, England: Sage.

Bourdieu, P. (1988). *Homo Academicus*. Stanford, CA: Stanford University Press.

Bracho, A., & Latino Health Access. (2000). Towards a healthy community … even if we have to sell tamales: The work of Latino Health Access. *Dulwich Centre Journal, 3*, 3–20.

Brigitte, Sue, Mem, & Veronika. (1997). Power to our journeys. Dulwich Centre Newsletter, 1, 25–34. Reprinted in C. White & D. Denborough (Eds.). (1998). *Introducing narrative therapy: A collection of practice-based writings* (pp. 203–215). Adelaide, Australia: Dulwich Centre Publications.

Bruner, E. M. (1986). Ethnography as narrative. In V. Turner & E. Bruner (Eds.), *The anthropology of experience* (pp. 139–155). Chicago: University of Illinois Press.

Bruner, J. (1986). *Actual minds, possible worlds*. Cambridge, MA: Harvard University Press.

Bruner, J. (1990). *Acts of meaning*. Cambridge, MA: Harvard University Press.

Byrne, A., Warren, A., Joof, B., Johnson, D., Casimir, L., Hinds, C., & Griffiths, S. (2011). 'A powerful piece of work': African and Caribbean men talking about the 'tree of life'. *Context,* (October), 40–45.

Casdagli, L., Christie, D., Girling, I., Ali, S., & Fredman, G. (in press). Evaluating the Tree of Life Project for Children and Young People living with Type 1 Diabetes at UCLH: An innovative way of engaging young people with diabetes. *Diabetes Care for Children and Young People*.

Chamberlain, S. (2004). A tale of narrative therapy. *Narrative Network News,* (September/October), 34–37.

Chamberlain, S. (2011). Narrative therapy: Challenges and community practices. In A. J. Lock & T. Strong (Eds.), *Discursive therapies*. Oxford, England: Oxford University Press.

Chamberlain, S., Foxwell-Norton, K., & Anderson, H. (Eds.). (2014). *Generation next: Becoming socially enterprising*. Melbourne, Australia: Oxford University Press.

Chatman, S. (1980). What novels can do that films can't (and vice-versa). In W. J. T. Mitchell (Ed.), *On narrative* (pp. 117–136). Chicago, IL: University of Chicago Press.

Clacherty, G. (2006). The world in a suitcase: Psychosocial support using artwork with refugee children in South Africa. *Participatory Learning and Action, 54*, 121–127.

Clacherty, G., Suitcase Storytellers, & Welvering, D. (2006). *The suitcase stories: Refugee children reclaim their identities*. Cape Town, South Africa: Double Storey Books.

Clayton, M., Fredman, G., Martin, E., Anderson, E., Battistella, S., Johnson, A., & Rapaport, P. (2012). Systemic practice with older people: Collaboration, community and social movement. *PSIGE Newsletter, 21*, 20–26.

Colorado, A., Montgomery, P., & Tovar, J. (2003). Creating respectful relationships in the name of the Latino family: A community approach to domestic violence. In Dulwich Centre Publications (Ed.), *Responding to violence: A collection of papers relating to child sexual abuse and violence in intimate relationships* (pp. 139–159). Adelaide, Australia: Dulwich Centre Publications.

Connell, R. W. (1987). *Gender and power: Society, the person and sexual politics*. Sydney, Australia: Allen and Unwin.

Couto, R. A. (1993). Narrative, free space, and political leadership in social movements. *The Journal of Politics, 55*(1), 57–79.

Damas, P., & Rayhan, I. (2004). *Vulnerability and poverty: What are the causes and how are they related?* (Unpublished term paper). Retrieved from: www.zef.de/fileadmin/downloads/forum/docprog/Termpapers/2004_3a_Philip_Rayan.pdf

Davies, B. (1993). *Shards of glass: Children reading and writing beyond gendered identities*. Sydney, Australia: Allen and Unwin.

Davis, V. (2017, February 24). *My meeting place: Re-arming ourselves with cultural knowledge, spirituality and community connectedness by Vanessa Davis* [Video file]. Retrieved from: dulwichcentre.com.au/my-meeting-place-re-arming-ourselves-with-cultural-knowledge-spirituality-and-community-connectedness-by-vanessa-davis/

Denborough, D. (1995a). Step by step: Developing respectful and effective ways of working with young men to reduce violence. *Dulwich Centre Newsletter*, (2&3), 73–89. Reprinted in C. McLean, M. Carey, & C. White (Eds.). (1996). *Men's ways of being* (pp. 91–115). Boulder, CO: Westview Press.

Denborough, D. (1995b) Becoming squarehead, becoming gubba. In L. Anderson (Ed.), *Bedtime stories for tired therapists* (pp. 162–178). Adelaide, Australia: Dulwich Centre Publications.

Denborough, D. (Ed.). (1996). *Beyond the prison: Gathering dreams of freedom*. Adelaide, Australia: Dulwich Centre Publications.

Denborough, D. (2001). Trying to find a founding father. *Dulwich Centre Journal, 1*, 7–9.

Denborough, D. (2002a). The Narrandera Koori Community Gathering. Retrieved from: dulwichcentre.com.au/articles-about-narrative-therapy/narrandera/

Denborough, D. (2002b). Community song writing and narrative practice. *Clinical Psychology, 17*, 17–24.

Denborough, D. (2005). A framework for receiving and documenting testimonies of trauma. *International Journal of Narrative Therapy and Community Work*, (3&4), 34–42. Reprinted in D. Denborough (Ed.). (2006). *Trauma: Narrative responses to traumatic experience* (pp. 115–131). Adelaide, Australia: Dulwich Centre Publications.

Denborough, D. (Ed.). (2006). *Trauma: Narrative responses to traumatic experience*. Adelaide, Australia: Dulwich Centre Publications.

Denborough, D. (2008). *Collective narrative practice: Responding to individuals, groups, and communities who have experienced trauma*. Adelaide, Australia: Dulwich Centre Publications.

Denborough, D. (2009). Some reflections on the legacies of Michael White: An Australian perspective. *Australian and New Zealand Journal of Family Therapy, 30*(2), 92–108. doi:10.1375/anft.30.2.92

Denborough, D. (2010a). *Kite of Life: From intergenerational conflict to intergenerational alliance*. Adelaide, Australia: Dulwich Centre Publications.

Denborough, D. (2010b). *Working with memory in the shadow of genocide: The narrative practices of Ibuka trauma counsellors*. Adelaide, Australia: Dulwich Centre Foundation.

Denborough, D. (Ed.). (2010c). *Raising our heads above the clouds: The use of narrative practices to motivate social action and economic development: The work of Caleb Wakhungu and the Mt Elgon Self-Help Community Project*. Adelaide, Australia: Dulwich Centre Publications.

Denborough, D. (2012). The Team of Life with young men of refugee backgrounds. *International Journal of Narrative Therapy and Community Work*, (2), 44–53.

Denborough, D. (2013). Healing and justice together: Searching for narrative justice. *International Journal of Narrative Therapy and Community Work*, (3), 13–17.

Denborough, D. (2014). *Retelling the stories of our lives: Everyday narrative therapy to draw inspiration and transform experience*. New York, NY: Norton.

Denborough, D. (2015, Feburary 25). *Narrative therapy charter of story-telling rights by David Denborough* [video file]. Retrieved from: dulwichcentre.com.au/narrative-therapy-charter-of-story-telling-rights-by-david-denborough/

Denborough, D., Koolmatrie, C., Mununggirritj, D., Marika, D., Dhurrkay, W., & Yunupingu, M. (2006). Linking stories and initiatives: A narrative approach to working with the skills and knowledge of communities. *International Journal of Narrative Therapy and Community Work*, (2), 19–51.

Denborough, D., & Preventing Prisoner Rape Project. (2005). Prisoner rape support package: Addressing sexual assault in men's prisons. *International Journal of Narrative Therapy and Community Work*, (2), 29–37.

Denborough, D., White, C., Claver, H. I. P., Freedman, J., & Combs, G. (2012), Responding to genocide: local knowledge and counterstories from genocide survivors in Rwanda. In C. Tatz (Ed.), *Genocide Perspectives*, Vol. 4. Sydney, Australia: UTS ePress.

Denborough, D., Wingard, B., & White, C. (2009). *Yia Marra: Good stories that make spirits strong – from the people of Ntaria/Hermannsburg*. Adelaide and Alice Springs, Australia: Dulwich Centre Publications and General Practice Network NT.

Denneny, M. (1984). Introduction. In M. Denneny, C. Ortleb, & T. Steele (Eds.), *The view from Christopher Street* (pp. 13–17). London, England: Chatto and Windus.

Derrida, J. (1981). *Positions*. Chicago, IL: University of Chicago Press.

Dulwich Centre. (Ed.). (1992) Some thoughts on men's ways of being [Special issue]. *Dulwich Centre Journal*, (3&4).

Dulwich Centre (Ed.). (2000) Living positive lives: A gathering for people with an HIV positive diagnosis and workers within the HIV sector [Special issue]. *Dulwich Centre Journal*, (4).

Dulwich Centre (Ed.). (2005a) Responding to trauma Part 1 [Special issue]. *International Journal of Narrative Therapy and Community Work,* (2).

Dulwich Centre (Ed.). (2005b) Responding to trauma Part 2 [Special issue]. *International Journal of Narrative Therapy and Community Work,* (3&4).

Dulwich Centre Community Mental Health Project. (1997). Companions on a journey: The work of the Dulwich Centre Community Mental Health Project. *Dulwich Centre Newsletter,* (1), 2–36.

Dulwich Centre Foundation. (2008). *Finding hidden stories of strength and skills: Using the Tree of Life with Aboriginal and Torres Strait Islander children* [DVD]. Adelaide: Dulwich Centre Publications.

Dulwich Centre Foundation. (2011). *Life-saving tips: Special skills and knowledge from young Muslim Australians.* Adelaide: Author.

Dulwich Centre Foundation International & International Women's Development Agency. (2013). *Narrative responses to human rights abuses: Sustaining women workers and honouring the survival skills of women from Burma/Myanmar.* Melbourne, Australia: International Women's Development Agency.

Durrant, M., & White, C. (Eds.). (1990). *Ideas for therapy with sexual abuse.* Adelaide, Australia: Dulwich Centre Publications.

Elhassan, O., & Yassine, L. (2017). Tree of Life with young Muslim women in Australia. *International Journal of Narrative Therapy and Community Work,* (3), 27–45.

Epston, D. (1986). Writing your history. *Family Therapy Case Studies, 1*(1), 13–18. Reprinted in D. Epston. (1989). *Collected papers* (pp. 129–134). Adelaide, Australia: Dulwich Centre Publications.

Epston, D. (1989a). *Collected papers.* Adelaide, Australia: Dulwich Centre Publications.

Epston, D. (1989b). Marisa revisits. In D. Epston, *Collected papers* (pp. 128–136). Adelaide, Australia: Dulwich Centre Publications.

Epston, D. (1998). *'Catching up' with David Epston: A collection of narrative practice-based papers published between 1991 and 1996.* Adelaide: Dulwich Centre Publications.

Epston, D. (2001). Anthropology, archives, co-research and narrative therapy. In D. Denborough (Ed.), *Family therapy: Exploring the field's past, present and possible futures* (pp. 177–182). Adelaide, Australia: Dulwich Centre Publications.

Epston, D. (2008). *Down under and up over: Travels with narrative therapy.* London, England: Association of Family Therapy.

Epston, D. (2011). Introduction. In D. Denborough (Ed.), *Narrative practice: Continuing the conversations* (pp. xxi–xxxviii). New York, NY: Norton.

Epston, D. (2014). Ethnography, co-research and insider knowledges. *International Journal of Narrative Therapy and Community Work,* (1), 65–68.

Epston, D., & White, M. (1990). Consulting your consultants: The documentation of alternative knowledges. *Dulwich Centre Newsletter,* (4), 25–35. Reprinted In D. Epston & M. White. (1992). *Experience, contradiction, narrative and imagination: Selected papers of David Epston and Michael White, 1989-1991* (pp. 11-26). Adelaide, Australia: Dulwich Centre Publications.

Epston, D., & White, M. (1998). A proposal for a re-authoring therapy: Rose's revisioning of her life, and a commentary by Kevin Murray. In: *'Catching up' with David Epston: A collection of narrative practice-based papers published between 1991 and 1996* (pp. 9–32). Adelaide, Australia: Dulwich Centre Publications.

Escobar, A. (1995). *Encountering development: The making and unmaking of the third world.* Princeton, NJ: Princeton University Press.

Esteva, G. (2010). Development. In W. Sachs (Ed.), *The development dictionary: A guide to knowledge as power* (pp. 1–23). London, England: Zed.

Flood, M. (1995). Activism 101. *XY: Men, Sex, Politics,* (Autumn), 22–24.

Fludernik, M. (1996). *Towards a 'natural' narratology.* New York, NY: Routledge.

Foucault, M. (1979). *Discipline and punish: The birth of the prison* (A. Sheridan, Trans.). New York, NY: Random House.

Foucault, M. (1983). Afterword. In H. L. Dreyfus, & P. Rabinow (Eds.), *Michael Foucault: Beyond structuralism and hermeneutics* (pp. 208–252). Chicago, IL: University of Chicago Press.

Foucault, M. (1984). *The history of sexuality* (Vol. 1). London, England: Peregrine.

Foucault, M. (1988). The political technology of individuals. In L. H. Martin, H. Gutman, & P. H. Hutton (Eds.), *Technologies of the self: A seminar with Michel Foucault* (pp. 161–175). Amherst: University of Massachusetts Press.

Foucault, M. (1997). *Ethics: Subjectivity and truth* (P. Rabinow, Ed.) New York, NY: New Press.

Fox, H. (2003). Using therapeutic documents: A review. *International Journal of Narrative Therapy and Community Work,* (4), 26–36.

Freedman, J., & Combs, G. (1996). *Narrative therapy: The social construction of preferred realities.* New York, NY: Norton.

Freeman, J., Epston, D., & Lobovits, D. (1997). *Playful approaches to serious problems: Narrative therapy with children and their families.* New York, NY: Norton.

Freire, P. (1973). *Pedagogy of the oppressed.* Ringwood, Australia: Penguin.

Freire, P. (1994). *Pedagogy of hope: Reliving Pedagogy of the oppressed.* New York, NY: Continuum.

Freire, P. (1999). Making history and unveiling oppression (D. Denborough & C. White, interviewers). *Dulwich Centre Journal,* (3), 37–39.

Freire, P. (2000). *Cultural action for freedom.* Boston, MA: Harvard Educational Review.

Freire, P., & Macebo, D. (1987). *Literacy: Reading the word and the world.* London, England: Routledge.

Ganz, M. (2011). Public narrative, collective action, and power. In S. Odugbemi & T. Lee (Eds.), *Accountability through public opinion: From inertia to public action* (pp. 273–289). Washington DC: World Bank.

Geertz, C. (1973). *The interpretation of cultures.* New York, NY: Basic.

Geertz, C. (1983). *Local knowledge: Further essays in interpretive anthropology.* New York, NY: Basic.

Gergen, K. J., & Gergen, M. M. (1983). Narratives of the self. In T. R. Sarbin & K. E. Scheibe (Eds.), *Studies in social identity* (pp. 254–268), New York, NY: Praeger.

Gergen, M. M., & Gergen, K. J. (1984). The social construction of narrative accounts. In K. J. Gergen & M. M. Gergen (Eds.), *Historical social psychology* (pp. 173–190). Hillsdale, NJ: Erlbaum.

German, M. (2013). Developing our cultural strengths: Using the 'Tree of Life' strength-based, narrative therapy intervention in schools, to enhance self-esteem, cultural understanding and to challenge racism. *Educational and Child Psychology, 30*(4), 75–99.

Gibson-Graham, J. K. (2006). *A postcapitalist politics.* Minneapolis, MN: University of Minnesota Press.

Goffman, E. (1959). *The presentation of self in everyday life.* Harmondsworth, England: Penguin.

Goffman, E. (1961). *Asylums: Essays in the social situation of mental patients and other inmates.* New York, NY: Doubleday.

Goffman, E. (1974). *Frame analysis.* Harmondsworth, England: Penguin.

Gordon, C. (Ed.). (1980). *Power/knowledge: Selected interviews and other writings 1972-1977 by Michel Foucault.* (C. Gordon, L. Marshall, J. Mepham, & K. Soper, Trans.). Harlow, England: Pearson.

Greer, G. (1970). *The female eunuch.* London, England: Paladin.

Grieves, L. (1997). From beginning to start: The Vancouver AntiAnorexia Anti-Bulimia League. *Gecko: A Journal of Deconstruction and Narrative Ideas in Therapeutic Practice,* (2), 78–88.

Hall, C., Baillie, D., Basangwa, D., & Atakunda, J. (2016). Brain gain in Uganda: A case study of peer working as an adjunct to statutory mental health care in a low income country. In R. White, S. Jain, D. Orr, & U. Read (Eds.), *The Palgrave handbook for global mental health: Sociocultural perspectives.* London, England: Palgrave MacMillan.

Hardy, B. (1968). Towards a poetics of fiction: An approach through narrative. *Novel: A Forum on fiction, 2*(1), 5–14.

Harrison, L. E., & Huntington, S. P. (Eds.). (2000). *Culture matters: How values shape human progress.* New York, NY: Basic.

Hegarty, T., Smith, G., & Hammersley, M. (2010). Crossing the river: A metaphor of separation, liminality, and reincorporation. *International Journal of Narrative Therapy and Community Work,* (2), 51–58.

Herman, D. (2002). *Story logic: Problems and possibilities of narrative.* Lincoln, NE: University of Nebraska Press.

Hernawan, B. J., & van den Broek, T. (1999). Dialog Nasional Papua, Sebuah Kisah 'Memoria Passionis': Kisah Ingatan Penderitaan Sebangsa. In *Tifa Irian.* Port Numbay: Jayapura.

Horton, M., Kohl, J., & Kohl, H. (1998). *The long haul: An autobiography.* New York, NY: Teachers College.

Hughes, G. (2014). Finding a voice through 'The Tree of Life': A strength-based approach to mental health for refugee children and families in schools. *Clinical Child Psychology and Psychiatry, 19*(1) 139–153.

Hung, S., & Denborough, D. (2013). Unearthing new concepts of justice: Women sexual violence survivors seeking healing and justice. *International Journal of Narrative Therapy and Community Work*, (3), 18–27.

Iliopoulou, G., Jovia, Kenny, Lucy, & Sandra. (2009). The tree of Life in a community context. *Context*, 105, 50–54.

Jacobs, D. (Ed.). (2003). *The Myles Horton reader: Education for social change.* Knoxville: University of Tennessee Press.

James, W. (1890). *The principles of psychology* (Vol. 1). New York, NY: Dover.

Jedlowski, P. (2001). Memory and sociology: Themes and issues. *Time Society, 10*(1), 29–44. doi:10.1177/0961463X01010001002

Jenkins, A. (1990). *Invitations to responsibility: The therapeutic engagement of men who are violent and abusive.* Adelaide, Australia: Dulwich Centre Publications.

Johnson, C. (2015). Reclaiming lives and language through the Tree of Life. In B. Wingard, C. Johnson, & T. Drahm-Butler (Eds.), *Aboriginal narrative practice: Honouring storylines of pride, strength and creativity* (pp. 15–23). Adelaide, Australia: Dulwich Centre Publications.

Kaminsky, M. (1992a). Introduction. In M. Kaminsky (Ed.), *Remembered lives: The work of ritual, storytelling, and growing older* (pp. 1–97). Ann Arbor: University of Michigan Press.

Kaminsky, M. (1992b). Myerhoff's 'Third Voice': Ideology and genre in ethnographic narrative. *Social Text,* (33), 124–144.

Kaminsky, M. (1993). Definitional ceremonies: Depoliticizing and reenchanting the culture of age. In T. R. Cole, W. A. Achenbaum, P L. Jakobi, & R. Kastenbaum (Eds.), *Voices and visions of aging: Toward a critical gerontology* (pp. 257–276). New York, NY: Springer.

Kimmel, M. (1987). *Changing men: New directions in research on men and masculinity.* Newbury Park, CA: Sage.

Kirkuk Center for Torture Victims & Dulwich Centre Foundation International. (2012). *Responding to survivors of torture and suffering: Survival skills and stories of Kurdish families.* Adelaide, Australia: Dulwich Centre Publications.

Kitzinger, C., & Perkins, R. (1993). *Changing our minds: Lesbian feminism and psychology.* New York, NY: New York University Press.

Kriewaldt, M. (1995). Diversity and difference. *XY: Men, Sex, Politics,* (Autumn), 25–27.

Landes, D. D. (2000). Culture makes almost all the difference. In L. E. Harrison & S. P. Huntington (Eds.), *Culture matters: How values shape human progress* (pp. 2–13). New York, NY: Basic.

Lanfer, P. T. (2012). *Remembering Eden: The reception history of Genesis 3: 22–24.* New York, NY: Oxford University Press.

Leger, M. F. (2016) Exploring the bicycle metaphor as a vehicle for rich story development: A collective narrative practice project. *International Journal of Narrative Therapy and Community Work,* (2), 17–35.

Lester, J. (2001). Coming home: Voices of the day. In B. Wingard & J. Lester (Eds.), *Telling our stories in ways that make us stronger* (pp. 1–9). Adelaide, Australia: Dulwich Centre Publications.

Lima, M. (2014). *The book of trees: Visualizing branches of knowledge.* New York, NY: Princeton Architectural Press.

Lobovits, D. H., Maisel, R. L., & Freeman, J. C. (1995). Public practices: An ethic of circulation. In S. Friedman (Ed.), *The reflecting team in action: Collaborative practice in family therapy* (pp. 223–256). New York, NY: Guilford.

Lock, A., Epston, D., & Maisel, R. (2004). Countering that which is called anorexia. *Narrative Inquiry, 14*(2), 275–301.

Lock, A., Epston, D., Maisel, R., & de Faria, N. (2005). Resisting anorexia/bulimia: Foucauldian perspectives in narrative therapy. *British Journal of Guidance and Counselling, 33*(3), 315–332.

Lowe, R. (1989). *Re-imagining family therapy: Choosing the metaphors we live by.* Paper presented at the New Zealand and Australian Family Therapy Conference, Christchurch, New Zealand.

Lowenthal, D. (1994). Identity, heritage, and history. In J. R. Gillis (Ed.), *Commemorations: The politics of national identity* (pp. 41–57). Princeton, NJ: Princeton University Press.

MacLeod, J. (2015). *Merdeka and the Morning Star: Civil resistance in West Papua.* Brisbane, Australia: University of Queensland Press.

MacLeod, J., & Whelan, J. (2015). *People power manual: Campaign strategy guide.* Brisbane, Australia: Pasifica and The Change Agency.

Madigan, S. (2011). *Narrative therapy.* Washington, DC: American Psychological Association.

Madigan, S., & Epston, D. (1995). From 'spy-chiatric' gaze to communities of concern: From professional monologue to dialogue. In S. Friedman (Ed.), *The reflecting team in action: Collaborative practice in family therapy* (pp. 257–276). New York, NY: Guilford.

Maisel, R., Epston, D., & Borden, A. (2004). *Biting the hand that starves you: Inspiring resistance to anorexia/bulimia.* New York, NY: Norton.

Malson, H., & Burns, M. (Eds.). (2009). *Critical feminist approaches to eating dis/orders.* London, England: Routledge.

Marsten, D., Epston, D., & Johnson, L. (2011). Consulting your consultants, revisited. *International Journal of Narrative Therapy and Community work,* (3), 57-71.

Mayer, F. W. (2014). *Narrative politics: Stories and collective action.* Oxford: Oxford University Press.

McAdam, E. (1998). The appreciative enquiry project. *Dulwich Centre Journal,* (2&3), 58–63.

McAdam, E., & Lang, P. (2010). *Appreciative work in schools.* London, England: Kingsham.

McFarlane, F., & Howes, H. (2012). Narrative approaches to group parenting work: Using the tree of life with 'hard-to-reach' parents. *Context, 123,* 22–25.

McLean, C., Carey, M., & White, C. (Eds.). (1996). *Men's ways of being.* Boulder, CO: Westview.

McLeod, J. (1997). *Narrative and psychotherapy.* London, England: Sage.

McLeod, J. (2004). The significance of narrative and storytelling in postpsychological counselling and psychotherapy. In A. Lieblich, D. P. McAdams, & R. Josselson (Eds.), *Healing plots: The narrative basis of psychotherapy* (pp. 11–27). Washington, DC: American Psychological Association.

McLeod, J. (2005). Counseling and psychotherapy as cultural work. In L. T. Hoshmand (Ed.), *Culture, psychotherapy and counseling: Critical and integrative perspectives* (pp. 47–63). Thousand Oaks, CA: Sage.

McLeod, J. (2007). Narrative thinking and the emergence of postpsychological therapies. In M. G. W. Bamberg (Ed.), *Narrative – State of the art* (pp. 237–245) Amsterdam, Netherlands: Benjamins.

McMenamin, D. (1999). Interviewing racism. In Dulwich Centre Publications (Ed.), *Extending narrative therapy: A collection of practice-based papers* (pp. 13–19). Adelaide, Australia: Dulwich Centre Publications.

Messerschmidt, J. W. (1993). *Masculinities and crime: Critique and reconceptualization of theory.* Lanham, MD: Rowman and Littlefield.

Morgan, A. (2000). *What is narrative therapy?: An easy-to-read introduction.* Adelaide, Australia: Dulwich Centre Publications.

Morgan, R. (Ed.). (1970). *Sisterhood is powerful: An anthology of writing from the women's liberation movement.* New York, NY: Vintage.

Morris, A. (1984). *The origins of the civil rights movement.* New York, NY: Free Press.

Murray, K. (1985). Life as fiction. *Journal for the Theory of Social Behaviour, 15*(2), 173–188.

Myerhoff, B. (1982). Life history among the elderly: Performance, visibility, and re-membering. In J. Ruby (Ed.), *A crack in the mirror: Reflective perspectives in anthropology* (pp. 99–117). Philadelphia: University of Pennsylvania Press.

Myerhoff, B. (1986). 'Life not death in Venice': Its second life. In V. Turner & E. Bruner (Eds.), *The anthropology of experience* (pp. 261–286). Chicago: University of Illinois Press.

Ncube, N. (2006). The Tree of Life Project: Using narrative ideas in work with vulnerable children in Southern Africa. *International Journal of Narrative Therapy and Community Work,* (1), 3–16.

Ncube-Mlilo, N. (2014, August 30). *Narratives in the suitcase by Ncazelo Ncube-Mlilo* [Video file]. Retrieved from: dulwichcentre.com.au/narratives-in-the-suitcase-by-ncazelo-ncube-mlilo/

Nelson, H. L. (2001). *Damaged identities, narrative repair.* Ithaca, NY; Cornell University Press.

Nelson, J., & Dunn, K. (2011). Bystander anti-racism: A review of the literature. *Analyses of Social Issues and Public Policy, 11*(1), 263–284.

Newman, D. (2008). 'Rescuing the said from the saying of it': Living documentation in narrative therapy. *International Journal of Narrative Therapy and Community Work,* (3), 24–34.

NiaNia, W., Bush, A., & Epston, D. (2017). *Collaborative and Indigenous mental health therapy: Tataihono – Stories of Maori healing and psychiatry.* New York, NY: Routledge.

Pietsch, T. W. (2013). *Trees of life: A visual history of evolution.* Baltimore, MD: Johns Hopkins University Press.

Polletta, F. (1999). 'Free spaces' in collective action. *Theory and Society, 28*(1), 1–38.

Portnoy, S., Girling, I., & Fredman, G. (2015). Supporting young people living with cancer to tell their stories in ways that make them stronger: The Beads of Life approach. *Clinical Child Psychology and Psychiatry, 21,* 255–267.

Pupavac, V. (2001). Therapeutic governance: Psycho-social intervention and trauma risk management. *Disasters, 25*(4), 358–372.

Pupavac, V. (2002a). Pathologizing populations and colonizing minds: International psychosocial programs in Kosovo. *Alternatives, 27,* 489–511.

Pupavac, V. (2002b). *Therapeutising refugees, pathologising populations: International psycho-social programmes in Kosovo* (New Issues in Refugee Research, Working Paper No. 59). Geneva, Switzerland: UNHCR.

Pupavac, V. (2006). *Refugees in the sick role: Stereotyping refugees and eroding refugee rights* (New Issues in Refugee Research, Research Paper No.128). Geneva, Switzerland: UNHCR.

Rao, V., & Walton, M. (Eds.). (2004). *Culture and public action.* Stanford, CA: Stanford University Press.

Reynolds, V. (2011). Resisting burnout with justice-doing. *International Journal of Narrative Therapy and Community Work,* (4), 27–45.

Rieniets, A. (1995). Souvenir. On *Fluently Helvetica* [CD]. Adelaide, Australia: Independent Production.

Rigney, A. (2013). History as text: Narrative theory and history. In N. Partner & S. Foot (Eds.), *The Sage handbook of historical theory* (pp. 183–201). London, England: Sage.

Roth, S., & Epston, D. (1996). Consulting the problem about the problematic relationship: An exercise for experiencing a relationship with an externalised problem. In M. Hoyt (Ed.), *Constructive therapies 2* (pp. 148–162). New York, NY: Guilford.

Rudland-Wood, N. (2012). Recipes for Life. *International Journal of Narrative Therapy and Community Work,* (2), 34–43.

Russell, S., & Carey, M. (2004). *Narrative therapy: Responding to your questions.* Adelaide, Australia: Dulwich Centre Publications.

Ryan, M. (2004). *Narrative across media: The languages of storytelling.* Lincoln, NE: University of Nebraska Press.

Sachs, W. (Ed.). (2010). *The development dictionary: A guide to knowledge as power* (2nd ed.). New York, NY: Zed.

Said, E., & Marranca, B. (1991). Criticism, culture, and performance: An interview with Edward Said. *Performing Arts Journal, 13*(1), 21–42.

Sawicki, J. (1991). *Disciplining Foucault: Feminism, power and the body.* New York, NY: Praeger.

Scott, J. C. (1990). *Domination and the arts of resistance: Hidden transcripts.* New Haven, CT: Yale University Press.

Segal, L. (1990). *Slow motion: Changing masculinity, changing men.* London, England: Virago

Selwyn College, Lewis, D., & Cheshire, A. (1998). Taking the hassle out of school: The work of the Anti-Harassment Team of Selwyn College, Dorothea Lewis and Aileen Cheshire. *Dulwich Centre Journal,* (2&3), 3–32.

Sen, A. (2004). How does culture matter? In V. Rao & M. Walton, (Eds.), *Culture and public action* (pp. 37–58). Palo Alto, CA: Stanford University Press.

Sen, A. (2006). *Identity and violence: The illusion of destiny.* New York, NY: Norton.

Silent Too Long. (1998). Your voices inspire mine. *Dulwich Centre Journal, 4,* 2–8.

Silent Too Long. (2000). Embracing the old, nurturing the new. *Dulwich Centre Journal,* (1&2), 62–71. Reprinted in Dulwich Centre Publications (Ed.). (2003), *Responding to violence: A collection of papers relating to child sexual abuse and violence in intimate relationships* (pp. 71–91). Adelaide, Australia: Author.

Silent Too Long. (2001). Trust. In Dulwich Centre Publications (Ed.), *Working with the stories of women's lives* (pp. 85–82). Adelaide, Australia: Dulwich Centre Publications.

Sliep, Y. (2005). A narrative theatre approach to working with communities affected by trauma, conflict and war. *International Journal of Narrative Therapy and Community Work,* (2), 47–52.

Sliep, Y., & CARE Counsellors. (1996). Pang' ono pang' onondimtolo – little by little we make a bundle. *Dulwich Centre Newsletter,* (3), 3–11. Reprinted in C. White & D. Denborough, (Eds.). (1998). *Introducing narrative therapy: A collection of practice-based writings* (pp. 141–156). Adelaide, Australia: Dulwich Centre Publications.

Sliep, Y., Weingarten, K., & Gilbert, A. (2004). Narrative theatre as an interactive community approach to health related interventions: Mobilizing community action. *Family Systems and Health, 22*(3), 306–320.

South Australian Council of Social Service, & Dulwich Centre. (1995). Speaking out and being heard: A report that documents the voices of mental health consumers and carers who took part in a joint project in 1995. *Dulwich Centre Newsletter,* (4), 3–56.

STOP. (n.d). What is stop? Retrieved from: www.stopviolenceeveryday.org/stop-2/

Stubbs, M. (1980). *Language and literacy: The sociolinguistics of reading and writing.* London, England: Routledge.

Swan, J. (2016, July 29) *Creating preferred family trees: Adjusting the recipe of collective narrative practices by Jennifer Swan* [Video file]. Retrieved from: dulwichcentre.com.au/creating-preferred-family-trees-adjusting-the-recipe-of-collective-narrative-practices-by-jennifer-swan/

Tamasese, K. (2002a). Honouring Samoan ways and understandings: Towards culturally appropriate mental health services. *International Journal of Narrative Therapy and Community Work,* (2), 64–71. Reprinted in C. Waldegrave, T. Tamasese, F. Tuhaka, & W. Campbell (Eds.). (2003). *Just Therapy – a journey: A collection of papers from the Just Therapy Team, New Zealand* (pp. 183–195). Adelaide, Australia: Dulwich Centre Publications.

Tamasese, K. (2002b). Multiple sites of healing: Developing culturally appropriate responses. In C. Waldegrave, K. Tamasese, F. Tuhaka, & W. Campbell (Eds.). (2003). *Just Therapy – a journey: A collection of papers from the Just Therapy Team, New Zealand* (pp. 197–200). Adelaide, Australia: Dulwich Centre Publications.

Timmel, S., & Hope, A. (1984). *Training for transformation: A handbook for community workers* (Books 1–3). Gweru, Zimbabwe: Mambo.

Tomm, K. (1989). Foreword. In M. White & D. Epston, *Literate means to therapeutic ends* (pp. 5–8). Adelaide, Australia: Dulwich Centre Publications.

Tse, K. H. (2016) Collective narrative practice with young people with Aspergers Syndrome who have experienced bullying. *International Journal of Narrative Therapy and Community Work*, (3), 8–20.

Tuhiwai Smith, L. (1999). *Decolonizing methodologies: Research and indigenous peoples*. London, England: Zed.

Turner, V. (1967). *The forest of symbols: Aspects of Ndembu ritual*. Ithaca, NY: Cornell University Press.

Turner, V. (1969). *The ritual process: Structure and anti- structure*. New York, NY: Aldine de Gruyter.

Turner, V. (1979). *Process, performance and pilgrimage: A study in comparative symbology*. New Delhi, India: Concept.

Turner, V. (1986). *The anthropology of performance*. New York, NY: PAJ.

Van Gennep, A. (1960). *The rites of passage*. Chicago, IL: The University of Chicago Press.

Varanda, W. (1999). 'Associação Minha Rua Minha Casa': My street my home association (D. Denborough, interviewer). *Dulwich Centre Journal*, (3), 20–23.

Waldegrave, C. (1990). Just Therapy. *Dulwich Centre Newsletter*, (1), 645. Republished in C. Waldegrave, K. Tamasese, F. Tuhaka, & W. Campbell (Eds.). (2003). *Just Therapy - a journey: A collection of papers from the Just Therapy Team, New Zealand* (pp. 3–61). Adelaide, Australia: Dulwich Centre Publications.

Waldegrave, C. (1998). The challenges of culture to psychology and postmodern thinking. In M. McGoldrick (Ed.), *Re-visioning family therapy: Race, culture and gender in clinical practice* (pp. 404–413). New York, NY: Guilford.

Waldegrave, C., Tamasese, T. Tuhaka, F., & Campbell, W. (Eds.). (2003). *Just Therapy - a journey: A collection of papers from the Just Therapy Team, New Zealand*. Adelaide, Australia: Dulwich Centre Publications.

Walls, D. (2015). *Community organizing: Fanning the flame of democracy*. Cambridge, England: Polity.

Watters, E. (2010). *Crazy like us: The globalisation of the American psyche*. Carlton, Australia: Scribe.

Weine, S. (2008). Testimony after catastrophe: Narrating the traumas of political violence. *Political Psychology, 29* (4), 627–630. doi:10.1111/j.1467-9221.2008.00657.x

Welch, S. (1990). *A feminist ethic of risk*. Minneapolis, MN: Fortress.

Wertsch, J. V. (2002). *Voices of collective remembering*. Cambridge, England: Cambridge University Press.

White, C. (2009). Where did it all begin? Reflecting on the collaborative work of Michael White and David Epston. *Context*, (October), 59–60.

White, C. (2011). Epilogue: Continuing conversations. In D. Denborough (Ed.), *Narrative practice: Continuing the conversations* (pp. 157–179). New York, NY: Norton.

White, C., & Denborough, D. (2005). *A community of ideas: Behind the scenes: The work of Dulwich Centre Publications*. Adelaide, Australia: Dulwich Centre Publications.

White, M. (1984). Pseudo-encopresis: From avalanche to victory, from vicious to virtuous cycles. *Family Systems Medicine, 2*(2), 150–160. doi:10.1037/h0091651

White, M. (1985). Fear busting and monster taming: An approach to the fears of young children. *Dulwich Centre Review*, 29–34. Reprinted in M. White (1989), *Selected Papers* (pp. 107–113). Adelaide, Australia: Dulwich Centre Publications.

White, M. (1986) Family escape from trouble. *Case Studies, 1*(1), 59–63. Reprinted in M. White (1989), *Selected Papers* (pp. 59–63). Adelaide, Australia: Dulwich Centre Publications.

White, M. (1987). Family therapy and schizophrenia: Addressing the 'in-the-corner' lifestyle. *Dulwich Centre Newsletter*, (Spring), 14–21. Reprinted in M. White (1989), *Selected Papers* (pp. 47–57). Adelaide, Australia: Dulwich Centre Publications.

White, M. (1988a). Saying hullo again: The incorporation of the lost relationship in the resolution of grief. *Dulwich Centre Newsletter*, (Spring), 7–11. Reprinted in M. White (1989), *Selected papers* (pp. 29–35). Adelaide, Australia: Dulwich Centre Publications.

White, M. (1988b). The process of questioning: A therapy of literary merit? *Dulwich Centre Newsletter*, (Winter), 8–14. Reprinted in M. White (1989), *Selected papers* (pp. 37–46). Adelaide, Australia: Dulwich Centre Publications.

White, M. (1988c). The externalizing of the problem and the re-authoring of lives and relationships. *Dulwich Centre Newsletter*, (Summer 1988/89), 3–21. Reprinted in M. White (1989), *Selected papers* (pp. 5–28). Adelaide, Australia: Dulwich Centre Publications.

White, M. (1989). Background. In M. White & D. Epston, *Literate means to therapeutic ends* (pp. 12–43). Adelaide, Australia: Dulwich Centre Publications.

White, M. (1991). Deconstruction and therapy. *Dulwich Centre Newsletter*, (3), 21-40. Reprinted in D. Epston & M. White (1992), *Experience, contradiction, narrative and imagination: Selected papers of David Epston and Michael White, 1989-1991* (pp. 109-151). Adelaide, Australia: Dulwich Centre Publications.

White, M. (1992). Men's culture, the men's movement, and the constitution of men's lives. *Dulwich Centre Newsletter*, (3&4), 33–53.

White, M. (1995a). Psychotic experience and discourse (K. Stewart, interviewer). In: M. White (Ed.), *Re-authoring lives: Interviews and essays* (pp. 112–154). Adelaide, Australia: Dulwich Centre Publications.

White, M. (1995b). Reflecting teamwork as definitional ceremony. In M. White (Ed.), *Re-authoring lives: Interviews and essays* (pp. 172–198). Adelaide, Australia: Dulwich Centre Publications.

White, M. (1995c). Therapeutic documents revisited. In M. White (Ed.), *Reauthoring lives: Interviews and essays* (pp. 199–213). Adelaide, Australia: Dulwich Centre Publications.

White, M. (1997). *Narratives of therapists' lives*. Adelaide, Australia: Dulwich Centre Publications.

White, M. (1999). Reflecting-team work as definitional ceremony revisited. *Gecko: A Journal of Deconstruction and Narrative Ideas in Therapeutic Practice*, (2), 55–82. Reprinted in M. White (Ed.). (2000). *Reflections on narrative practice: Essays and interviews* (pp. 59–85). Adelaide, Australia: Dulwich Centre Publications.

White, M. (2000). Re-engaging with history: The absent but implicit. In M. White (Ed.), *Reflections on narrative practice: Essays and interviews* (pp. 35–58). Adelaide, Australia: Dulwich Centre Publications.

White, M. (2001a). Folk psychology and narrative practice. *Dulwich Centre Journal,* (2), 1–37.

White, M. (2001b). The narrative metaphor in family therapy. An interview (D. Denborough, interviewer). In D. Denborough (Ed.), *Family therapy: Exploring the field's past, present and possible futures* (pp. 131–138). Adelaide, Australia: Dulwich Centre Publications.

White, M. (2003). Narrative practice and community assignments. *International Journal of Narrative Therapy and Community Work,* (2), 17–55.

White, M. (2004a). Narrative practice, couple therapy and conflict dissolution. In M. White (Ed.), *Narrative practice and exotic lives: Resurrecting diversity in everyday life* (pp. 1–41). Adelaide, Australia: Dulwich Centre Publications.

White, M. (2004b). Working with people who are suffering the consequences of multiple trauma: A narrative perspective. *International Journal of Narrative Therapy and Community Work,* (1), 45–76. Reprinted in D. Denborough, (Ed.). (2006). *Trauma: Narrative responses to traumatic experience* (pp. 25–85). Adelaide, Australia: Dulwich Centre Publications.

White, M. (2006a). Fostering collaboration – between families and children, and between child protection services and families. In M. White & A. Morgan (Eds.), *Narrative therapy with children and their families* (pp. 121–136). Adelaide, Australia: Dulwich Centre.

White, M. (2006b). Responding to children who have experienced significant trauma: A narrative perspective. In M. White & A. Morgan (Eds.), *Narrative therapy with children and their families* (pp. 85–97). Adelaide, Australia: Dulwich Centre Publications.

White, M. (2006c). Working with people who are suffering the consequences of multiple trauma: a narrative perspective. In D. Denborough (Ed.), *Trauma: Narrative responses to traumatic experience* (pp. 25–85). Adelaide, Australia: Dulwich Centre Publications.

White, M. (2007). *Maps of narrative practice.* New York, NY: Norton.

White, M. (2011). Revaluation and resonance. In Denborough, D. (Ed.), *Narrative practice: Continuing the conversations* (pp. 123–134). New York, NY: Norton.

White, M., & Epston, D. (1989). *Literate means to therapeutic ends.* Adelaide, Australia: Dulwich Centre Publications.

White, M., & Epston, D. (1990). *Narrative means to therapeutic ends.* New York, NY: Norton.

Wingard, B. (1996a). Grief: Remember, reflect, reveal. *Dulwich Centre Newsletter,* (3), 30–35. Reprinted in B. Wingard & J. Lester (Eds.). (2001). *Telling our stories in ways that make us stronger* (pp. 45–55). Adelaide, Australia: Dulwich Centre Publications.

Wingard, B. (1996b). Introducing 'Sugar'. *Dulwich Centre Newsletter,* (3), 26–29.

Wingard, B. (2010). A conversation with Lateral Violence. *International Journal of Narrative Therapy and Community Work,* (1), 13–17.

Wingard, B., & Dulwich Centre Foundation. (Eds.). (2015). *Stories of hope for Aboriginal children, families and culture.* Adelaide, Australia: Dulwich Centre Publications.

Wingard, B., & Lester, J. (2001). *Telling our stories in ways that make us stronger.* Adelaide, Australia: Dulwich Centre Publications.

Wolf, W. (2005). Pictorial narrativity. In D. Herman, M. Jahn & M-L, Ryan, (Eds.) *Routledge encyclopedia of narrative theory.* New York, NY: Routledge.

WOWSafe. (2002). Seeking safety and acknowledgement. *International Journal of Narrative Therapy and Community Work,* (1), 70–74. Reprinted in Dulwich Centre Publications (Ed.). (2003). *Responding to violence: A collection of papers relating to child sexual abuse and violence in intimate relationships* (pp. 129–138). Adelaide, Australia: Dulwich Centre Publications.

Yuen, A., & White, C. (2007). *Conversations about gender, culture, violence and narrative practice: Stories of hope and complexity from women of many cultures.* Adelaide, Australia: Dulwich Centre Publications.

CPSIA information can be obtained
at www.ICGtesting.com
Printed in the USA
LVHW031806231121
704247LV00014B/1939

9 780648 154501